Clara Hannah Kerr

# Origin and development of the United States Senate

Clara Hannah Kerr

**Origin and development of the United States Senate**

ISBN/EAN: 9783337150969

Printed in Europe, USA, Canada, Australia, Japan

Cover: Foto ©Suzi / pixelio.de

More available books at **www.hansebooks.com**

THE

# ORIGIN AND DEVELOPMENT

OF THE

# UNITED STATES SENATE

BY

CLARA HANNAH KERR, PH.D.

---

ITHACA, N. Y.
ANDRUS & CHURCH
1895

# TABLE OF CONTENTS.

## CHAPTER I.



## CHAPTER II.



## CHAPTER III.



## CHAPTER IV.



## CHAPTER V.



## CHAPTER VI.

# PREFACE.

In the following study an effort has been made to trace the development of the United States senate from the time that a second house was first proposed in the convention of 1787 to the present. In this discussion especial attention has been paid to the way in which the senate has exercised the powers granted to it by the constitution, and to the ways in which, either by an increase or a decrease of those powers, it has deviated from the purpose of the framers of the constitution. In doing this the three functions exercised by that body, legislative, executive and judicial, have been separately treated.

It has been impossible to obtain a full knowledge of the proceedings of the senate during its early days, as the debates were not reported and the sessions, for some time, were held in secret. Our chief sources of information regarding the period are the "Annals of Congress" and the "Senate Journal." These are supplemented by the "Journal of Maclay," covering the period of the First Congress, and the writings of the early statesmen, especially those of Washington, John Adams, Jefferson, Hamilton and Madison.

The same difficulty exists throughout for the executive proceedings, as the executive sessions are still held in secret, and none of the debates have been made public, except in the few instances in which the injunction of secrecy has been removed from them. As the "Executive Journal" since 1869 has not been published, it is still more difficult to obtain an adequate knowledge of the executive proceedings since that date.

A list of the more important sources of information consulted in the preparation of this paper, including all those cited in the foot notes, is given at the end. Following established precedents, the document known as the "Pinckney Plan" has several times been cited, although the genuineness of that document is now seriously discredited.

The work has been done under the direction of Professor Moses Coit Tyler, to whose suggestions and assistance I am much indebted. I am also indebted to the Honorable Henry Cabot Lodge for aid while making personal observations of the senate, and to Mr. A. R. Spofford for help while using the Library of Congress.

C. H. K.

*Cornell University,*
*Ithaca, New York,*
*July, 1895.*

# THE ORIGIN AND DEVELOPMENT OF THE UNITED STATES SENATE.

## CHAPTER I.

### THE FORMATION OF THE SENATE IN THE CONVENTION OF 1787.

THE states, in adopting the articles of confederation which created a government in which all legislative power was vested in a single house, had departed from nearly all of their traditions of government. At that time, the division of the legislative power between the house of lords and the house of commons was considered an essential part of the English system; and, in all of the colonies except Pennsylvania, two houses had been developed, and were provided for by all of the state constitutions except those of Georgia and Pennsylvania. It was, therefore, but natural in framing a new form of government to replace that of the articles of confederation, which had proved inadequate, that a legislature of two branches should have been thought of. Both Randolph's and Pinckney's plans, introduced immediately after the organization of the convention, provided for two houses; and two days later the convention decided, without debate, Pennsylvania alone voting against it, in favor of such a distribution of the legislative power. Later, however, after the arrival of the New Jersey delegates, who wished only the amendment of the articles of confederation, the question was again considered, and New York and Delaware voted with New Jersey for a legislature of a single branch.

It being decided that there was to be a second house, the convention next proceeded to determine the manner in which its members should be chosen. During the colonial period, in the royal colonies the councillors were regularly appointed by the king, and in the proprietary colonies by the proprietor; while in the popular colonies they were either chosen by the general legislature, as in Massachusetts, or directly by the voters, as in Rhode Island and Connecticut. In the formation of the state constitutions the more popular method of election of Rhode Island and Connecticut was followed by most of the states.[1]

Each of the three plans submitted to the convention, however, provided for a secondary election: Pinckney's for an election by the lower house, Randolph's by the lower house from nominations made by the state legislatures, and Hamilton's for a choice by electors chosen by the people, as in Maryland. A proposal by Mr. Read of Delaware removed the choice still farther from the people by giving to the executive the appointment of senators from a certain number nominated by the individual legislatures. This, however, was too monarchical to meet with approval, and was not supported; though later Gouverneur Morris, who at this time was absent, went still farther and declared that he was in favor of the simple appointment of senators by the executive.

The direct election of senators by the people, proposed and warmly supported by the committee to whom the Randolph plan was referred, was objected to on the grounds that the people could not safely be entrusted with the power, and because it would give to the landed interests an undue preponderance; and the plan adopted by many of the states in choosing members to the congress of the confederation, namely, choice by the state

[1] Under the first constitutions of S. C. and N. H. the members of the upper house were chosen by those of the lower; and in Maryland by electors chosen by the people.

legislatures, was agreed upon, it being held that the sense of the people could be better collected in this way, and that thus the most distinguished characters would be chosen. It was also pointed out that this method had the advantage of connecting the state and national governments.

In the debates over the formation of the constitution, the point which caused the most discussion was the method of representation in the two branches of congress. Though the colonies had an equal voice in the continental congress, it had not been granted without a struggle,[1] and during the debates over the question several compromises had been suggested. That of Sherman of Connecticut, who proposed that "the vote should be taken two ways; call the Colonies, and call the individuals, and have a majority of both,"[2] was a foreshadowing of the plan of the senate and house of representatives.

The delegates from Delaware had been forbidden to vote for any constitution which should not provide for the equality of representation of the states, and there were others strongly in favor of that plan. Proposals for the representation of the states in accordance with their importance and in accordance with property[3] were not well supported. The method of representation for the lower branch was first decided, the great struggle being over the plan to be adopted in the senate.

The possibility of different methods of representation in the two houses was evidently in the mind of Dickinson when, in the course of the discussion over the method of impeachment of the president, he said that he hoped that each state would retain an equal vote in at least one

[1] Works of J. Adams, II, 499.

[2] Works of J. Adams, II, 499.

[3] Representation in the state legislatures of Massachusetts and New Hampshire was based upon this principle.

branch of the national legislature;[1] but it was Sherman of Connecticut who, when both parties seemed bent upon having their own way, proposed granting representation of the states in proportion to their inhabitants, in one branch, and equal representation in the other.[2] His proposition was well supported by his colleague, but at that time no one else spoke in favor of the plan. It satisfied neither the small states nor the large ones, and it led to a discussion so violent that at one time there was danger of the convention's dissolving without accomplishing anything. Dr. Franklin then came forward urging the necessity of compromise. The matter was referred to a committee, who reported substantially the plan of Sherman. Many, seeing the necessity of a compromise, though by no means satisfied with the plan proposed, supported it; and the vote when taken stood five to four, with one state divided.[3]

All agreed that the senate ought to be so constituted as to be a check on the lower house, but there was a disagreement as to the means to be adopted to secure this end. Gouverneur Morris, having in mind, doubtless, the house of lords, thought that, for this purpose, dignity and permanence were necessary. He therefore wished to have the second branch composed of men of large property, an aristocracy who, from pride, would sustain consistency. To make them completely independent, he wished them chosen for life.[4] Hamilton's plan embodied the same idea, but it met with no success, for the people dreaded above all things the creation of an aristocracy. The councils of the colonies had, in general, been composed of the men of the most wealth and importance in the colony; and stood in social rank next to the governor, especially in the royal colonies, where they were

[1] Elliot, V, 149.
[2] *Ibid.*, V, 179.
[3] *Ibid.*, V, 316.
[4] *Ibid.*, I, 475.

appointed by the king during good behavior. They had constantly been objects of suspicion; and therefore, in the state constitutions, five years was the longest term of a senator,[1] while a majority of the states elected their senators annually. In the convention, the length of term proposed varied from a life tenure, urged by those who regarded the British constitution as the best of models, to a single year, a plan urged by the New England delegates, and especially those of Connecticut, who declared that their constituents would never consent to give up their annual elections. A short term of office was urged by the strong states' rights men also; for they feared that, if the term of service were long, the senators would make their home at the capitol city, and, forgetting their dependence and becoming alienated, would neglect the interests of the state which sent them.

At first the term of office was fixed at five years,[2] as a happy medium between the life tenure which, it was feared, would make the senators regardless of the wishes of the people, and a shorter term which would not be sufficient to secure permanency and consistency in the legislative business. Later, it was fixed at six years, one third going out each year.[3] Rotation was first suggested by Mr. Pinckey, and, when proposed later by Mr. Gorham, met with no opposition. An effort to introduce a property qualification, which existed in seven of the state constitutions,[4] failed; but the recognition of the greater ability required of a senator was shown by making the age qualification of a senator thirty years; and, in view of the fact that they were to have an

[1] The Maryland senators held office five years; Delaware's three; Virginia's four; New York's four.

[2] Elliot, I, 451.

[3] Rotation was adopted for the provisional council of Pennsylvania in the "Frame of Government" of 1782–3, and for the state council. It was also provided for the senates in the state constitutions of New York, Delaware, and Virginia.

[4] In Mass., Md., Del., N. C., N. J., N. Y., N. H.

agency in the formation of treaties, the term of citizenship required was fixed at nine years.

It was pretty generally agreed that the duties which were to be assigned to the senate could be best performed by a small number. Gouverneur Morris favored three representatives from each state, for he thought if there were but two, and a majority a quorum, the senate would be too small to entrust with the important duties which had been assigned to it. This number was objected to on the ground of expense, and because it would be difficult for the more remote states to send so many; and, on the motion for two from each state, Maryland alone voted against it.[1]

It has been said that a long term for senators was opposed by the supporters of states' rights on the ground that it would diminish the influence of the states. The same reason led them to oppose, though unsuccessfully, the voting *per capita* instead of by states, and the payment of the senators out of the national treasury; the difference of opinion on all these points being due to different ideas regarding the office of the senate. The states' rights party, who wished the senate to represent the states, advocated their payment by the states that they might not become independent of them; while the national party, who wished the senate to be representative of national and not state interests, advocated the payment of senators from the national treasury. The national party prevailed, and the payment of senators was left to the general government. A proposal to fix the salary was discarded on account of the change of values, and a motion which provided that the compensation of senators and representatives should be the same was withdrawn when it was pointed out that this would be unfair, as senators would have to remain longer from home and so would be obliged to remove their families.[2]

[1] Elliot, V, 356-357.
[2] Elliot, V, 425-427.

The powers which the senate was to have were at first but vaguely defined. Thus, Mr. Randolph's plan, as first submitted and as amended in the committee of the whole, made no distinction as to the powers to be granted to the two houses. The Pinckney plan gave the originating of all money bills to the house of delegates, and to the senate the sole power of declaring war, making peace, and appointing ambassadors; while Hamilton's, which was introduced about a month later, gave to the senate the sole power of declaring war; of advising and approving treaties; of approving or rejecting all nominations, except the heads or chiefs of the departments of war, finance, and foreign affairs.[1]

Although the upper house of every state except Connecticut, Rhode Island, and North Carolina was restricted by its constitution from originating money bills, a proposal in the early part of the convention, before the manner of representation was decided upon, to limit the United States senate in a similar manner, was negatived. Later, when it had been decided that the states were to be equally represented in the second branch, it was proposed, as a compensation to the large states, to give to the first branch of the legislature the exclusive right of originating "all bills for raising and appropriating money and for fixing salaries," and to forbid the senate's altering or amending them;[2] and, though some of the representatives of the large states, among whom were Mr. Madison and Mr. Wilson, declared that they saw no concession in this, it was agreed to by a majority of two states. This decision was very unsatisfactory to many, and the subject was again brought up for consideration. Those who were in favor of the clause as it then stood, supported it because senators were not the direct representatives of the people, and because it was feared that

[1] In several of the states the upper house could not even amend money bills. It was so in S. C., Md., Va., N. J.

[2] Elliot, V, 274.

the senate would sit constantly, and so be able to mature plans during the recess and force them upon the house.[1] Another reason, according to Colonel Mason, for restricting the upper house was that "it could already sell the country by means of its treaties."[2] It was finally agreed to amend the clause so that it would read: "All bills for raising revenue shall originate in the House of Representatives, but the Senate may propose or concur with amendments."[3]

One of the greatest defects in the government formed under the articles of confederation was the lack of an adequate war power; and, as before noticed, in the plans of Pinckney and Hamilton the power of declaring war was entrusted to the senate. Pinckney urged that the senate would be the best repository of this power, as it would be better acquainted with foreign affairs, was representative of the states, and was a smaller body. Moreover it would be singular to entrust the power of making war to one body, and that of peace to another. His reasoning, however, was ineffectual; the majority of the convention being unwilling to entrust so important a power to the senate alone.

The same objection was raised to giving to the senate alone the treaty-making power. A proposal to give it to the president met with no more favor, and it was finally agreed that the treaty-making power should be given to the president, by and with the advice and consent of two-thirds of the senators present. The two-thirds vote was objected to by many, as the minority would thus be able to control the majority, and it was urged that, as the president was to be associated with the senate in the negotiation of treaties, that would be a sufficient check.[4] There were, on the other hand, those

[1] Elliot, V, 415.
[2] *Ibid.*, 427.
[3] *Ibid.*, 529.
[4] *Ibid.*, 524.

who would have still further restricted the power of the senate; and the conventions of North Carolina and Virginia which adopted the constitution proposed that, for ceding territorial rights, the consent of three-fourths of the senate should be required.[1]

The trial of impeachments seems to have been confided to the senate less because it was thought to be preeminently fitted for the work than because there was no other body better suited to it.[2] Both Randolph's and Pinckney's plans gave the trial of impeachments to the national judiciary, and it was thus reported by the committee of detail. Not until near the end of the convention was it proposed to substitute the senate in the trial of the impeachment of the president.[3] It was urged in favor of the change that a small number of judges, indebted to the president for their appointments, could scarcely be impartial and might be corrupted;[4] and it was finally decided to give to the senate the trial, not only of the president, but of all officers liable to impeachment.

As, in the state governments, all the appointments were not made in the same manner, so, in the national convention, it seems not to have been intended at first to place the appointment of all officers in the power of one person or body. Randolph's plan mentioned only the judges, the appointment of whom he would have given to the national legislature. Pinckney's plan gave to the

[1] Elliot, IV, 245; III, Virginia, 660.

[2] Elliot V, 508, and Federalist, No. 65. In the latter Hamilton upholds the plan adopted by the convention, not by showing that the senate was a body eminently fitted for the work, but by pointing out the defects in the other plans proposed, and concluding that the duty might better be assigned to the senate than to any other body.

[3] Elliot, V, 507. The constitutions of Mass. and Del., and the second constitution of N. H. gave the trial of impeachments to the upper house; while in S. C. the trial of impeachments was given to the senate and all judges not members of the lower house; and in New York to the senate, chancellor, and judges of the supreme court.

[4] *Ibid.*, 528, 529.

senate the appointment of judges of the supreme court, ambassadors, and all ministers to foreign ports; and to the president, with the consent of the senate, all other appointments. While Hamilton would have given the appointment of all officers to the president, and to the senate, the confirmation of all but the heads of the departments. A proposal to refer certain appointments to the legislatures or executives of the several states,[1] as well as a confirmation of certain appointments by an equal vote of the states,[2] met with little support. The chief debates were over the manner of appointment of the judicial officers and ambassadors. Mr. Gorham suggested "that the judges be appointed by the executive, with the advice and consent of the second branch, in the mode prescribed by the constitution of Massachusetts." "This mode," he said, "had been practised long in that country, and was found to answer perfectly well."[3] Mr. Madison suggested a confirmation by two-thirds of the senate. Both of these as well as an appointment by the president and by the national legislature were voted down: the appointment of judges and also of ambassadors was given to the senate; and to the president, the appointment of all officers not otherwise provided for. The first draft of the constitution regulated appointments in this manner, and it was not until the first of September that a committee of eleven, to whom the postponed parts of the constitution had been referred, reported the clause substantially as it now stands.[4] To the objection of Mr. Wilson that this mode would destroy the responsibility of the executive,

[1] Elliot, V, 475.

[2] *Ibid.*, 266.

[3] *Ibid.*, 328. Mr. Gorham's recollection seems to have been at fault for the constitution then in force in Massachusetts says: "All judicial officers shall be appointed by the Governor by and with the advice and consent of the Council," which was not the second branch of the legislature.

[4] *Ibid.*, 507.

Gouverneur Morris replied "that, as the President was to nominate, there would be responsibility, and as the Senate was to concur, there would be security."[1] Mr. Gerry, on the other hand, said: "The idea of responsibility in the nomination to office is chimerical. The President cannot know all characters, and can therefore always plead ignorance."[2] There was, however, very little debate, and, after a slight change, the clause was adopted.

To the senate had been left the choice of its president, as well as its other officers, until a successor for the president was provided, when, in order to give him something to do, he was made president of the senate. This plan was advocated because otherwise some member of the senate would have to preside, and would thus be deprived of his vote except in the case of a tie.[3] It was objected to as being an encroachment on the rights of the senate, and because it mingled too much the legislative and executive powers.[4] Mr. Gerry, thinking that there would be between the president and vice president a close intimacy, said that they "might as well put the president himself at the head of the legislature." Gouverneur Morris, with truer insight, saw that the relations of the two would not be such as to warrant any fear.[5]

Two other subjects deserve mention from the influence which a different decision of them would have had on the senate. The first of these is the manner of electing the president of the United States. Many methods were suggested, two of which would have changed considerably the relations of the president and senate. One providing for an election by the national legislature, which

[1] Elliot, V, 523.

[2] *Ibid.*, 523.

[3] *Ibid.*, 522.

[4] *Ibid.*

[5] *Ibid.*, 522.

was the plan adopted in most of the state constitutions,[1] was at first the favorite and was adopted. Later, when this was reconsidered and the choice of the president given to electors, it was proposed that, in case of two candidates having an equal number of votes or of no candidate having a majority, the election should be made by the senate out of the five highest candidates. As it was thought that, in the choice by electors, there would seldom be anyone who would have a majority, it was believed that this was really giving the election to the senate; and the fear that this would make the president dependent on the senate, lead to corruption, and lay the foundation for an aristocracy, led to its rejection and the substitution of the house for the senate.[2]

The other subject to be noticed is the proposal for an executive council, to whom, instead of the senate, should be given the confirmation of appointments made by the president. Many objected to the latter method because of the mingling of the legislative and executive functions, and because they thought that it would render necessary the continuous session of the senate, a circumstance which would be expensive and might be dangerous. Moreover, they thought the senate too large a body for that purpose. That there should have been many in favor of an executive council is not strange, for one was provided for by the constitutions of nearly all the states, and, as Colonel Mason said, "in rejecting a council to the President an experiment was about to be tried which the most despotic government had never ventured upon."[3] The delegates to the con-

[1] It was so in Delaware, Maryland, Virginia, New Jersey, North Carolina, South Carolina under both the first and second of its constitutions, and in New Hampshire under its first constitution. In Pennsylvania the executive officer was elected by the assembly and council, in Georgia by the assembly and in all the other states by the people.

[2] Elliot, V, 507, 520-524.

[3] *Ibid.*, V, 525.

vention, however, preferred to adopt the plan of the colonies in the earlier days, of combining in the upper house the duties of a council to the president and of a branch of the legislature.

There was a wide difference of opinion as to the relative powers of the president, senate, and house of representatives, in the government as finally constituted. First, in regard to the relation of the president and senate; there were, on the one side, those who, like Martin, believed that the senate, through their desire for the emoluments and the offices which the president could give, would become subservient to him;[1] on the other side, there were those who, like Madison, believed that the power of the senate to try impeachments and to confirm nominations would make the president dependent upon it.[2] As regards the relative powers of the two houses, there was the same difference of opinion. Thus, there were many who, either on account of the immense powers given to the senate, or the small number of its members, or their long continuance in office,[3] or for all these reasons, fearedthat the senate would be able to destroy any balance in the government and to accomplish whatever usurpations it wished on the liberties of the people. Colonel Mason even went so far as to say that if a coalition should be established between the president and the senate they could overthrow the government.[4] On the other side there were some who thought that the restriction placed upon the senate in regard to bills for raising revenue rendered it almost useless as a part of the legislature.[5] A more moderate view is set forth by Hamilton in the "Federalist," where he says: "Against the force of the immediate representatives of

[1] Elliot, I, 361.
[2] Elliot, V, 528.
[3] Elliot, II, 286.
[4] Elliot, V, 513.
[5] Elliot, I, 367.

the people, nothing will be able to maintain even the constitutional authority of the senate, but such a display of enlightened policy and attachment to the public good as will divide with that branch of the legislature the affections and support of the entire body of the people themselves."[1]

It was pretty generally agreed that the senate, from the manner of its election, would be composed of men of greater knowledge and broader information than the house; and that their proceedings would be marked by more coolness, system, and wisdom than those of the popular branch. There were also many who, thinking that the senators would be repeatedly re-elected and would reside at the capitol city, feared that they would form a class by themselves and so lay the foundation of an aristocracy; and this fear, which led to the proposal of an amendment in the New York convention, lasted for some time after the government had gone into operation.

[1] Federalist, No. 63.

## CHAPTER II.

### ELECTION OF SENATORS AND ORGANIZATION OF THE SENATE.

THE constitution framed by the convention and finally adopted, provided that "The times, places, and manner of holding elections for Senators and Representatives shall be prescribed in each State by the legislature thereof; but the Congress may, at any time, by law make or alter such regulations, except as to the places of choosing Senators."[1] This privilege congress did not avail itself of until 1866. In the meantime, the manner of choosing its senators was regulated by each state, the senators of some states being chosen by the two houses sitting separately, and others by a joint meeting of the two houses;[2] but in either case a majority was always considered necessary to elect, until 1866, when the New Jersey legislature, in joint session, decided that a plurality should elect. The senator so chosen was refused a seat in the senate, and this case led to the passage of the law regulating the mode of election. This law provided first for a *viva voce* election in each house by a majority of all the votes cast. If the same person did not receive a majority in both houses, or if either house had failed to elect, then, on the following day, the two houses, in joint assembly, were to proceed in the same manner as before to the choice of a senator.[3]

[1] Article I, section IV.

[2] In 1866 there were sixteen or seventeen states in which the senators were so elected (Congr. Globe, 1st Sess., 39th Congr., p. 1571, statement of Mr. Johnson.) though there were some distinguished men, like Sumner and Kent, who thought that this was contrary to the spirit of the constitution. (Sumner, Works, X, 381, 382.)

[3] Revised Statutes, Sects., 14, 15, 16.

The right conferred on the senate of judging of the elections, qualifications, and returns of its own members, and of punishing them for disorderly behavior, and, with the concurrence of two-thirds, of expelling a member,[1] has been frequently exercised, there having been, between 1789 and 1885, sixty-eight election cases considered by the senate,[2] and ten senators expelled, beside those who, at the breaking out of the war, were either expelled, or their names stricken from the lists, or their seats declared vacant. The cases of senators who were appointed by the governor are important as interpretations of the power, granted by the constitution to the state executive, to make temporary appointments when "vacancies happen by resignation or otherwise, during the recess of the legislature of any State."[3]

The decision in 1797 in the case of Kensey Johns of Delaware established the principle that the executive could not make an appointment to fill a vacancy if a session of the legislature had been held since the vacancy existed.[4]

In 1809 it was decided[5] that a senator, appointed by a governor during the recess of the legislature to hold office until the meeting of the next legislature, should hold his seat, after the meeting of the legislature, until the choice of a successor; while in 1850 it was also held that he should keep his seat until his successor had signified his acceptance of his election by the presentation of his credentials.[6] In 1853 this was further modified by the decision in the case of Samuel Phelps, who was appointed by the governor during the recess of the legis-

[1] Article I, section V.

[2] Sen. Misc. Docs., 49th Congr. 1st Sess., No. 47.

[3] Art. I, sect. 3.

[4] Sen. Misc. Docs., 1st Sess., 49th Congr., No. 47, p. 1. This decision was reaffirmed in 1853, *Ibid.*, p. 23.

[5] *Ibid.*, p. 4. In the case of Samuel Smith.

[6] This decision has since governed the action of the senate. (2d Sess., 31st Congr., Sen. Reports, No. 269.)

lature to fill a vacancy. Afterwards the state legislature met and adjourned without electing a senator. Phelps continued to occupy his seat during the remainder of the session of congress after the adjournment of the state legislature and also at a special session; but, when congress again met in December and he attended, his right to do so was questioned and decided in the negative.[1]

The right of the governor to make appointments to fill vacancies caused by the expiration of terms of office, as well as to make appointments to fill vacancies in unfinished terms, was not questioned until 1825 when a senator so appointed was declared not to be legally entitled to his seat but, as neither the debates nor the reasons for the decision are recorded, it is impossible to tell whether the decision was made on this ground or because the appointment was made in advance of the vacancy.[2] In favor of the first view are the numerous examples during the next fifty years of cases in which, under the same circumstances, vacancies have been allowed to exist until the meeting of the legislature,[3] as also the report of a committee on a somewhat similar case in 1837, which states the decision to have been made on this ground and to have been generally acquiesced in. In support of the other view are quotations from Story[4] and the "National Intelligencer"[5] which would seem to show that Mr. Lanman's right to a seat in the senate was denied on the ground that the governor could not make an appointment in anticipation of a vacancy. In 1879 and again in 1885 it was held that the governor had a right to make an appointment to fill

[1] 49th Congress 1st Sess., Sen. Misc. Docs., No. 47, p. 17.
[2] *Ibid.*, pp. 28, 31.
[3] 49th Congr., 1st Sess., Sen. Misc. Docs., No. 47, p. 29.
[4] Commentaries, § 727, note.
[5] March 8th, 1825.

a vacancy occasioned by the expiration of a term of a senator.[1]

The question whether the right of the senate to judge of the "elections, qualifications, and returns" of its own members gave it the power to admit when and how it pleased senators from the seceeded states, occupied much of the time of the Thirty-ninth Congress. Finally a resolution was adopted, in the senate by a vote of 29 to 18, which declared, in order to close agitation, that no senator or representative should be admitted into either branch of congress from any of the said states until congress declared such states to be entitled to representation.[2]

According to Hamilton it was to be expected from the choice of senators by the state legislatures, who themselves would be select bodies of men, that they would be chosen with peculiar care and judgment;[3] and that those elected would be men most distinguished for their abilities and virtue.[4] It was likewise expected that this method would have the advantage of removing the choice from the activity of party zeal. Indeed the choice by the state legislatures seems to have been looked upon with favor pretty generally; and whereas, in the first congresses, numerous resolutions were introduced for amendments to shorten the term of office, to prevent naturalized citizens from being chosen senators, to prevent one indebted to the United States or entrusted with the management of the money of the United States or direction of any bank from being a senator, and to prevent members of congress from being eligible to civil office, no motion seems to have been made to change the method of election.

[1] 49th Congr. 1st Sess., Sen. Misc. Docs., No. 47, pp. 26, 36.
[2] Congr. Globe, 1st Sess., 39th Congr., pp. 1143, 1147.
[3] Federalist, No. 27.
[4] *Ibid.*, No. 64.

The wished for removal of senatorial elections from party politics and popular prejudices obtained to a certain extent at first. Thus Gallatin, a strong republican and a representative of a republican district, was elected senator from Pennsylvania by a Federalist legislature, and this without his being a candidate by his own motion or that of his friends;[1] and Adams and Pickering were chosen senators by a Massachusetts legislature a few months after they had been defeated in an election for representatives,[2] which shows a state of affairs far different from the present, when a Nebraska senator recently resigned his position because the party majority in the state legislature had changed and he was no longer in accord with it.

A more important departure from the original idea regarding the election of senators is to be found in the gradual change from an indirect election to one which, in many cases, is practically direct. As early as 1851, when Sumner was elected senator, it seems that the idea of his candidacy was present in the state elections;[3] and since then candidates for the state legislature have frequently been pledged in advance to vote for a particular person as senator; and one constitution even contains a provision in accordance with which the legislature may provide for the expression by the electors of their preference for United States senator at the election next preceding the expiration of the term of a senator.[4]

The failure of the constitution in this respect is one of the prominent reasons urged in favor of a change in the method of election. Another reason is the corruption practised in the election of senators. This also is no new thing. In 1867, when Conkling was a candidate for sen-

[1] Stevens, Gallatin, p. 98.
[2] Life of Pickering, IV, 52, 53.
[3] Sumner, Works, II, 426.
[4] That of Nebraska of 1875.

ator, he wrote that he might have had from New York $200,000 to use in securing his election;[1] while *Harper's Weekly* in 1870 asserted that votes for senators in Rhode Island were bought at the rate of five dollars a head.[2] Federal patronage also is frequently employed to control the elections. This corruption, which is used in the election of the members of the state legislature, in the caucus, and in the action of the state legislature, has become a great evil. So stubborn and so eager are the contests at times that the election of senators has been known to occupy an entire session of the legislature. The demand for popular election of senators has been made by the legislatures of many of the states[3] and in the platforms of numerous party conventions. Such a demand was made by California and Iowa as early as 1874.[4] The house of representatives has twice passed, by the requisite two-thirds vote, a resolution for the proposed amendment,—in the 52nd Congress almost unanimously. These resolutions were quietly pigeon-holed in the senate; and similar resolutions, introduced in the senate, have served no purpose other than to give the mover an opportunity to gain popularity with his constituents by making a speech; and, although nearly every congress witnesses the introduction of such resolutions, there seems to be no immediate probability or even possibility of their passing the senate.

In its organization the senate has the advantage of the house in that, ordinarily, it does not have to choose a presiding officer; and that, even when it does, the office of president *pro tempore* being of slight importance as compared with that of speaker of the house, his election is of correspondingly less difficulty. The independence of the vice president, of the senate,

[1] Life of Conkling, p. 287.

[2] Nov. 26th, p. 755.

[3] Ill., Ind., Calif., Id., Ia., Kan., Ky., La., N. Y., Or., Wis.

[4] 43rd Congr., 1st Sess., Sen. Misc. Docs., Nos. 66, 69.

and its consequent inability, in any way, to control him, are undoubtedly the chief reasons why the senate always has done, and still continues to do for itself things which, in the house, are confided to the presiding officer. Even the right of preserving order, which is generally considered inherent in the duties of any presiding officer, has, at times, been questioned. The rules of the First Congress prescribed the course of procedure when a senator was called to order, but did not say who was to exercise the power.[1] The presiding officer, however, had, without question, been accustomed to exercise it, until the winter of 1826, when Vice President Calhoun decided that the right to call to order on questions touching the latitude or freedom of debate belonged exclusively to the members of the senate and not to the chair.[2] This gave rise to much discussion as to the position of the vice president in the senate and whence he derived his powers. Some, like John Quincy Adams, held that they were derived from the constitution, and others that they were dependent upon the rules and usages of the senate.[3] A proposal in 1828 for the amendment of the rules brought on another long discussion, and it was finally decided, two to one, to change the rules so as to read: "When a member shall be called to order by the President or a Senator," etc.[4]

[1] The rules of the First Congress on the subject were as follows: Rule 16: "When a member shall be called to order, he shall sit down until the President shall have determined whether he is in order or not: every question of order shall be decided by the President without debate; but if there be a doubt in his mind, he may call for the sense of the Senate." Rule 17: "If a member be called to order for words spoken, the exceptionable words shall be immediately taken down in writing, that the President may be better enabled to judge of the matter."

[2] Congressional Debates, vol. II, p. 573.

[3] Calhoun, Works, vol. VI, pp. 322 ff.

[4] Congr. Deb., 1st Sess., 20th Congr., vol. IV, Part I, pp. 340, 341. At the same time it was agreed, only two voting against it, that "every question of order shall be decided by the President, without debate, subject to appeal to the Senate."

The rule as amended, however, did not declare, as does for example that of the house of representatives, that the presiding officer should call to order, and a question arose as to whether the duty was more imperative on the chair than on any member of the house. Mr. Fillmore, calling attention to this in 1850, stated that he had concluded that, though under the rule the authority of the chair and of senators to call to order was equal, yet the duty was more imperative on the chair, and he should feel bound to discharge it accordingly.[1] However, Mr. Bright, a few years later, when acting as presiding officer, held that the rules did not authorize him to call a senator to order.[2] This decision was severely criticized, and led to the amendment of the rules so as to leave no doubt that it was imperative on the presiding officer to preserve order.[3]

The vice president can exercise but little influence on legislation, except through the power of the casting vote; and, as it has seldom happened that parties were equally divided in the senate, he has rarely had occasion to use it.[4] In the convention, when a council for the president was under discussion, it was suggested that the president of the senate, the speaker of the house, the chief justices of the supreme court, and the heads of departments should compose it;[5] and Adams considered his exclusion from the cabinet as a want of personal respect.[6]

[1] Congr. Globe, 1st Sess., 31st Congr., p. 632.

[2] *Ibid.*, 34th Congr., 1st Sess., p. 1483.

[3] The rule reads: "If any member, in speaking or otherwise, transgress the rules of the Senate, the Presiding Officer shall, or any member may, call to order; and when a member shall be called to order by the President, or a Senator, he shall sit down, and shall not proceed without leave of the Senate. And every question of order shall be decided by the President, without debate, subject to an appeal to the Senate; and the President may call for the sense of the Senate on any question of order." (1st Sess., 34th Congr., pp. 1477, 1484.)

[4] It was most considerable during the First Congress.

[5] Elliot, V, p. 462.

[6] Jefferson, however, regarded a share in the executive deliberations as inconsistent with his legislative duties.

Had Washington, in accordance with the desire of Adams, summoned him, as vice president, to the cabinet meetings, it is probable that the influence of both the president and vice president in the senate, especially since the change in the manner of election, so that the president and vice president are members of the same party, would have been greater than it now is.

The attendance of the vice president has varied much in accordance with circumstances and the will of the occupant of the office. After the passage of the law of March first, 1792, giving the succession to the presidency to the president *pro tempore*, in case there were no vice president, and after him to the speaker of the house, it became customary for the vice president to retire at least a few days before the end of the session, to give an opportunity for the election of a president *pro tempore*, that the succession to the presidency might not be endangered;[1] it being maintained that the president *pro tempore* held office over a recess of the senate, provided the vice president had not appeared in the senate since his election.[2]

The constitution provides for the choice of a president *pro tempore* in the absence of the vice president. In 1820 provision was also made by rule for filling the chair temporarily, it being provided that "the Vice President, or President of the Senate *pro tempore*, shall have the right to name a member to perform the duties of the Chair; but such a substitution shall not extend beyond

[1] The change in the succession to the presidency in 1886 made this no longer necessary.

[2] This was questioned in the 2d Sess. 39th Congr. (p. 380), though the presidents *pro tempore* of the preceding sessions, in the absence of the vice president at the opening of the session, had, with but four exceptions, presided, (1st Sess. 44th Congr., Sen. Reports, No. 3, p. 3). This practice was upheld by the chair. In the first session 44th Congress, (p. 377), a resolution which declared the office of president *pro tempore* of the senate to be held at the pleasure of that body was adopted.

an adjournment."[1] This rule was interpreted by some so as to limit the exercise of this power to cases in which the presiding officer was present in the senate chamber, and by others to extend to an appointment by him when not present. The first case in which objection seems to have been made to an appointment by the presiding officer in his absence was in 1845. The objection was withdrawn after some discussion in which attention was called to the case of Mr. Southard, who, for several days, had made such appointments.[2] The next session, however, a similar circumstance arising, the senate voted to proceed to the election of a president *pro tempore*, and the man designated by the vice president was chosen by the senate.[3] In 1856, on a similar occasion, the senate again unanimously elected the man designated by the presiding officer to take his place.[4] In 1879 such an appointment by the vice president passed without question, but in 1882 the senate again questioned the right, and, after some debate, adjourned, in order to avoid a decision.[5] At the next session, in the revision which the rules underwent, the power to make such an appointment was expressly conferred on the president *pro tempore*, no mention being made of the vice president.[6]

Until recently the tenure of office of the president *pro tempore* has been held to be dependent upon the vice president and to cease with his return to the senate.[7] This interpretation of the clause of the constitution which reads: "The Senate shall choose a President *pro tempore* in the absence of the Vice President," was not even questioned until 1861, when a resolution to reverse

[1] No. 22 of those adopted in 1820.

[2] Congr. Globe, 1st Sess., 29th Congr., p. 96.

[3] *Ibid.*, 2d Sess., 29th Congr., pp. 161, 162.

[4] *Ibid.*, 1st Sess., 34th Congr., pp. 1368, 1369.

[5] Congr. Record, 1st Sess., 47th Congr., pp. 4449-4454.

[6] *Ibid.*, 1st Sess., 48th Congr., pp. 160, 168, 237.

[7] Congr. Record, 1st Sess., 51st Congr., p. 2145, for list of cases.

the practice was introduced and debated, but not voted on.[1] When next it was brought up, the presidential succession had been changed so as to exclude the president *pro tempore*, and this seems to have influenced some to reverse the practice. Those who favored the change did so because of the greater convenience, and those opposing it did so on the ground that it was unconstitutional, since the term was fixed by the constitution.[2]

The right of the senate to control of the president *pro tempore* as well as the other officers of the senate, and, in consequence, the right to remove him and elect another at any time, though questioned, has always been upheld by the majority.[3]

Prior to 1824 the tenure of all the other officers of the senate was during good behavior. It was then provided that the secretary of the senate, sergeant-at-arms, door keeper, and assistant door keeper should be elected at the first session of every congress.[1] This rule remained in force until 1849,[2] when, on account of the inconveniences of such frequent elections, it was repealed, and an attempt to renew it in the Thirty-second Congress failed.[3] The Democratic party remaining in control of the senate until 1861, there were of course no changes in the officers for party reasons; but when, in that year, the Republicans obtained a majority, they at once proceeded to change certain of the officers of the senate.

Although this action seems to have been dictated by party motives only, the spoils system was not fully introduced. For some time afterwards the acting secretary

[1] Congr. Globe, 1st Sess., 37th Congr., p. 436.

[2] Congr. Record, 1st Sess., 51st Congr., p. 2153.

[3] *Ibid.*, 1st Sess., 44th Congr., Sen. Report, No. 3, p. 7. Also Congr. Record, 1st Sess., 44th Congr., p. 373, and 47th Congr., special, pp. 519 ff.

[4] Annals of Congr., 1st Sess., 18th Congr., p. 140.

[5] Congr. Globe, 2d Sess., 30th Congr., p. 490.

[6] *Ibid.*, 1st Sess., 32d Congr., p. 62.

was a Democrat,[1] and when the Democrats again came into power in 1879 thirty of the one hundred and twenty offices of the senate were filled by Democrats, some of whom had held over from the previous Democratic administration, while others had been chosen by the Republican senate. With the return of the Democrats to power in 1879 a sweeping change in the senate offices was made, the spoils system being fully introduced.[2]

In the early days of the senate, the vice president having taken his seat, or, he being absent, a president *pro tempore* having been elected, and the other officers of the senate having been chosen, the organization of the senate was completed; for there were at first no standing committees to be chosen. By an act of August sixth, 1789, a joint standing committee on enrolled bills, composed of two members from the house and one from the senate, was created;[3] and in 1806 a senate standing committee on engrossed bills was added.[4] At the same time it was provided that, "When any subject or matter shall have been referred to a select committee, any other subject or matter of a similar nature, may, on motion, be referred to such committee."[5] During the next session, in obedience to an act making appropriations for the purchase of books, a joint standing committee on the library was created;[6] and, at the succeeding congress, a standing committee to audit and control the contingent expenses of the senate was provided for.[7] These were

[1] The secretary, Mr. Dickens, was prevented by the infirmities of age from attending, and the chief clerk, a Democrat, performed the duties of the secretary until finally, on the advice of Mr. Dickens, a new election was held and a republican chosen. (Congr. Globe, 1st Sess., 37th Congr., p. 119.)

[2] Congr. Record, 1st Sess., 46th Congr., pp. 48–60.

[3] Senate Journal, 1st Sess., 1st Congr., p. 54.

[4] Rule 22.

[5] Rule 14.

[6] Sen. Jour., 2d Sess., 9th Congr., vol. IV, p. 114, Dec. 17, 1806.

[7] *Ibid.*, 1st Sess., 10th Congr., vol. IV, p. 191, Nov. 4, 1807.

the only standing committees appointed prior to 1816, when the number of select committees had become so large[1] and the inconveniences of frequent balloting had become so considerable, it was agreed that, thereafter, eleven standing committees should be appointed at the beginning of each session.[2] These were: The committees on foreign relations, on finance, on commerce and manufactures, on military affairs, on the militia, on naval affairs, on public lands, on the judiciary, on post offices and post roads, on pensions, and on claims. The two standing committees before mentioned were continued. The committee for the District of Columbia was added almost immediately after.[3] A committee on Indian affairs was created in 1819,[4] and one on roads and canals in 1820.[5] Other standing committees have been added as the need for them has appeared, until at the second session of the Fifty-second Congress there were forty-six standing committees to be appointed before the organization of the senate was completed.

The manner of appointment has been changed several times. The first rules provided for the election of all committees by ballot, a plurality of votes electing. It would, however, appear from the Journals that the rule was frequently set aside, for often instead of the usual form, "Ordered, That . . . . be a committee for . . . ," which would apply to any method of choosing committees, the appointment of a committee is noted thus:

"On motion,

"*Ordered*, That . . . be a committee . . . ," which would seem to indicate that the committee was

[1] Between 90 and 100 were appointed at the 1st Sess., 14th Congr. (3d Sess., 37th Congr., Sen. Misc. Docs., No. 42, p. 3.)

[2] Sen. Jour., 2d Sess., 14th Congr., p. 38.

[3] *Ibid.*, 49, 56.

[4] Sen. Jour., 1st Sess., 16th Congr., p. 65.

[5] *Ibid.*, p. 145, 148.

not chosen by ballot, but that it was accepted by the senate on the motion of one of its members.[1]

The standing committees, however, were for many years regularly chosen by ballot in accordance with the rule. From 1823 to 1833 the rules on the subject were changed several times, the senate apparently seeking a means by which it could avoid the tediousness of balloting and yet not allow the appointment of its committees to pass from its control.

In the first session of the Seventeenth Congress, the vice president being absent, a motion was made for the appointment of the committees by the presiding officer, but the vice president attending before the motion came to a vote, it was postponed. At the next session of congress, the vice president being again absent and his illness rendering his attendance improbable, the rule was changed so as to read: "All committees shall be appointed by the presiding officer of this House, unless specially ordered otherwise by the Senate." The last clause was probably added to make it possible, if the vice president should attend, to return at once to the former practice. The first session of the Nineteenth Congress, Vice President Calhoun attending, was allowed to appoint the committees; but before the end of the session a motion was made and carried, with only two dissenting voices, to return to the earlier practice;[2] and, at

[1] Mr. Breeze said that between 1789 and 1820 it was not customary for the senate to choose its own committees (1st Sess., 29th Congr., p. 21), and a rule given by Mr. Maclay which may have embodied the practice of the senate reads: "When a commitment is agreed upon, the President (of the Senate) shall take the sense of the Senate as to the manner of appointing the committee, whether by motion from the Senate, nomination from the chair, or by ballot; which shall take place accordingly." (Rule 13.)

[2] Congr. Debates, 1st Sess., 19th Congr., pp. 571, 572. It was asserted at the time that the change was not made because Vice President Calhoun had abused the power but on general principles; but Williams in his "Statesman's Manual" says that the change was made because of the improper use made by Mr. Calhoun of his power. (I, p. 656.)

the next session, before the election of committees, a change was made in the rules so as to provide for the election of the chairman of every committee separately and by a majority vote, and then for the election of the other members of each committee by a single ballot and a plurality vote.[1]

In 1828 the rule was again changed so as to give the appointment of the committees to the president *pro tempore*, if there was one, leaving the rule as before, in case the vice president was in the chair.[2] The reason of this distinction was said to be the irresponsibility of the vice president to the senate.[3]

This rule also was found unsatisfactory, for, in the first session of the Twenty-third Congress, the political majority in the senate having changed since the last session, the president *pro tempore*,[4] chosen at the previous session, was of the opposite party from the present majority. The rule was, therefore, changed and the appointment of the committees restored once more to the senate under the former rule, which has never been changed since;[5] except that in the rules adopted in the second session of the Forty-fourth Congress, the words "unless otherwise ordered" were inserted. Thus it is seen that the rules of the senate have provided for the choice of its committees by ballot during all but about seven years. Though since 1833 the rules have always provided for the choice of committees by ballot, they have been set aside much more frequently than followed. For

[1] Congr. Deb., 2d Sess., 19th Congr., p. 3.

[2] Sen. Journal, 2d Sess., 20th Congr., p. 51. The vice president was absent at the opening of the next two sessions, some thought designedly (Congr. Deb., 1st Sess., 23d Congr., 22), the rule being construed as an intimation that the senate desired the vice president to remain away until after its organization. Calhoun, however, denied that he had purposely been absent. (1st Sess., 23d Congr., p. 19.)

[3] Congr. Deb., 1st Sess., 23d Congr., p. 20.

[4] Hugh L. White.

[5] Congr. Globe, 1st Sess., 23d Congr., p. 20.

a time, whenever the vice president was absent, the appointment of the committees was almost invariably left to the president *pro tempore*.[1] Once, also, the appointment of all the committees was given to the vice president;[2] and another time, after the election of four of the chairmen, the appointment of the other members of the committees was left to the vice president.[3]

At the first session of the Twenty-ninth Congress, for the first time, a part of the committees were accepted by resolution;[4] and at the next session, after the chairmen of six of the committees had been chosen by ballot, a list agreed upon by both sides of the senate, in which the chairman of each committee and a majority of its members were of the same party as the majority of the senate, was read and adopted;[5] a way being thus found at last by which the senate could avoid the tediousness of balloting, and yet retain the control of the committees in its own hands. Since that time, with few exceptions, it has been the custom to move to suspend the

[1] At the third session of the 25th Congress (Congr. Globe., 16), and the first session of the 26th Congress (Congr. Globe, 50, 51), and the second session of the same Congress (Congr. Globe, 2, 12), the president *pro tempore* appointed all the committees but the chairman of the committee on commerce. At the first session of the 27th Congress (Congr. Globe, p. 11), the chairmen of the committees were chosen by the senate, but the appointment of the other members was given to the president *pro tempore*. At the third session of the 27th Congress (Congr. Globe, 38–40), the first session of the 28th Congress (Congr. Globe, pp. 5, 22), the second session of the same Congress (Congr. Globe, 8, 12), and the second session of the 31st Congress (Congr. Globe, p. 7), the committees were appointed by the president *pro tempore*.

[2] Congr. Globe, 2d Sess., 25th Congress, pp. 9, 12.

[3] *Ibid.*, 1st Sess., 25th Congr., 14, 16. Proposals for such a course made later were rejected. (Congr. Globe, 1st Sess., 29th Congr., pp. 19–21; 2d Sess., 29th Congr., 19.)

[4] Congr. Globe, 1st Sess., 29th Congr., p. 66.

[5] *Ibid.*, 2d Sess., 29th Congr., pp. 19, 30.

rules, and then to adopt a list of the committees decided upon in caucus.[1]

It would seem that the representation of both parties on the committees was no new thing, for Mr. King, who had served in the senate since the adoption of the constitution, stated in 1844 that it was the invariable practice.[2] On the other hand, Jefferson, in his "Parliamentary Manual" says that the British practice was to refer a bill to a committee all of whom favored it;[3] and, as he does not say that the practice of the senate was different, one is justified in inferring that it was the same. With the establishment of standing committees it would of course be impossible to know in advance exactly what bills were to be referred to each committee, and therefore impossible to follow the principle laid down by Jefferson. It may be, therefore, that it was then the present practice was established, and that it was of the standing committees only which Mr. King was thinking when he spoke of the practice in the matter. When the rule was followed and the committees were chosen by ballot, a plurality making a choice, unless some previous arrangement were made, the result was very uncertain;[4] but, with the introduction of the practice of adopting by resolution lists of committees previously made out and

[1] Exceptions to this practice are found in Congr. Globe: 2d Sess., 36th Congr., p. 23; 1st Sess., 31st Congr., 39, 45; 2d Sess., 31st Congr. p. 7; 1st Sess., 34th Congr., p. 18; 3d Sess., 37th Congr., p. 1554; 2d Sess., 45th Congr., p. 56; 3d Sess., 46th Congr., 14; 2d Sess., 47th Congr., p. 23.

[2] Benton, Thirty Years' View, II, pp. 335, 336.

[3] Section, XXVI.

[4] Mr. Hickey, Chief Clerk of the senate, in a report in 1863 said regarding this that it had been found that, without a previous consultation and arrangement, by the plurality principle, all the members of the committees, except the chairman, for whose election a majority was required, might be obtained by a united minority, contrary to the will of the majority; and that, on the other hand, with such an arrangement on the part of the majority, the minority might be entirely excluded from the committees. (3d Sess., 37th Congr., Sen. Reports, No. 42, p. 32.)

decided upon in caucus, there was no more difficulty on that score. Not only have the minority generally been represented on the committees, but, as a rule, the majority, after having made out a list of the committees, assigning their own members to the positions desired and leaving blanks for the minority to fill out, have sent this list to the minority for its action;[1] and Mr. Pendleton said in the Forty-seventh Congress that it had become the accepted custom for the majority of the senate to seek conference with the minority, to discuss with them not only the members of the minority who should be placed on each committee, but also regarding the number of representatives which the minority should have and the committees which they should entirely control.[2]

The practice in regard to the chairmanship of committees has not been uniform. Up to 1827, when it was provided that, for the election of the chairman of a committee, a majority should be required, while for the other members of the committee a plurality of votes only, there is no mention of a chairman in the rules of the senate as given in the "Senate Journal"; but Mr. Maclay says that the chairman of a committee was the senator of the most northerly state of those from which the members of the committee were taken. There seems, however, to be reason for doubting the correctness of this rule.[3]

[1] 3d Sess., 37th Congr., Special, p. 1554, statement of Mr. Saulsbury; 1st Sess., 38th Congr., 15, 16.

[2] Special Sess., 47th Congr., p. 16.

[3] Rule 12, Journal of Maclay. If this rule was observed it seems strange that it should have received no notice from the statesmen of the time, in their letters or writings, and that Jefferson should not have mentioned it in his "Parliamentary Manual," where he says in regard to the committees of parliament: "The clerk may deliver the bill to any member of the committee. But it is usual to deliver it to him who is first named." Moreover, Jefferson says that the chairman of the committee makes the report, but an examination of the "Senate Journal" shows that, generally, the person who reported the

The usual custom was to continue senators on the same committee, unless they desired change, and to promote no one over them; and the same way with the chairmen.[1] This custom has sometimes led to the possession of all the important places by senators from one district, as in the Thirty-seventh Congress, when, of the twenty-two committees, the chairmanship of eleven, and of these three of the most important, belonged to New England. Party politics, however, have been allowed to come in to a certain extent. In the second session of the Thirty-ninth Congress three distinguished chiefs were stricken from their places as chairmen and assigned the foot of their committees, although the committees did not have charge of matters of a political nature.[2] The removal of Mr. Sumner from the chairmanship of the committee on foreign affairs by his own party, because of his opposition to the president, is another example of departure from the rule. Mr. Cameron, his successor, was, however, entitled by seniority to the place if a vacancy should occur.[3]

The opportunity for corruption and jobbery which is offered by the application of seniority of service in one case and not in another, led to a proposal in the Fifty-third Congress, which, however, was rejected, that unless otherwise ordered "the committees of the Senate shall be organized with reference to the equality of the states, and that seniority of service shall give preference in the assignment of committees and chairmanships."

Of the forty-six standing committees of the senate, at the second session of the Fifty-third Congress, twenty-

bill was the one first mentioned on the committee, and he was not always the representative of the most northern state represented on the committee, though he very frequently was.

[1] Congr. Globe, 1st Sess., 36th Congr., p. 178; Blaine, Twenty Years in Congress, I, 323; 3d Sess., 37th Congr., Sen. Misc. Docs., No. 42.

[2] Congr. Globe, 2d Sess., 39th Congr., p. 520.

[3] Blaine, Twenty Years, II, 503, note.

one met regularly once a week, the others having no regular time of meeting but coming together when called by the chairman.

The number of members on the standing committees has varied. Three was the usual number prior to 1818 when the number was raised to five for all but two committees,[1] these being still composed of but three members. Since then the number of members on the various committees has been frequently changed and now the number varies from three to thirteen, nine being the most usual number. Each senator usually serves on from four to six committees. The meetings of the committees are ordinarily secret, though they may be made public.

Frequently special subjects are referred to sub-committees or individuals to investigate and report to the committee. The committee may be authorized to summon witnesses and to take evidence. The majority report of the committee is not signed, it being considered as the report of the whole committee. With the majority report are usually printed the views of the minority, each member of the minority being privileged to set forth his views.

The usual custom of the senate has been for the members of the committee of the opposite parties to consider the bills together. Recently, however, a tendency has been manifested to adopt the practice followed to a considerable extent in the house, of the majority and minority holding no conference on the subject. Thus, in the Forty-ninth Congress, a report was submitted by a majority of the committee which the minority first heard on the morning that the report was made to the senate;[2] and in the second session of the Fiftieth Congress the tariff substitute was prepared by the Republican

[1] Rules of 1820, No. 30.

[2] Congr. Record, 1st Sess., 49th Congr., p. 1584.

majority of the senate committee.[1] Sometimes, when there was need of haste, as in the second session of the Twenty-fifth Congress, a bill has been reported by a committee within twenty-four hours after its receipt, although the senate had been in session all the time, and the committee did not have leave to sit during the session, the bill having been separately considered by each member at his desk.[2]

The authorization of a committee to sit during the recess was unusual in the early days,[3] but it has now become quite common. The early committees did not employ clerks, but in 1849 one was granted to the committee on printing[4] and soon after all the other committees obtained them.[5] Each committee has its calendar and keeps a record of its proceedings.

The influence of committees on legislation has steadily increased from the early days when there were no standing committees, and motions were introduced on leave, a committee being raised to prepare a bill embodying the motion, until the present time. This is due to the increase in the amount of business to be done, which made it necessary constantly to rely more and more on committees. As early as 1855 it was said in the senate that more work was done in the committees than in the senate;[6] and in 1857 Mr. Hamlin said: "It is through committees to a very great extent—to much the greatest extent—that the business of the Senate is prepared and presented to the Senate for action."[7] The bills which are

[1] Congressional Record, p. 304.

[2] Congr. Globe, 2d Sess., 25th Congr., p. 384.

[3] The first instance was that of a committee appointed to investigate the affairs of the United States bank. Benton, II, p. 305.

[4] 1st Sess., 31st Congr., p. 61.

[5] In 1855 nineteen committees employed clerks and two years later all but four committees were allowed them. (1st Sess., 35th Congr., p. 158.) Now all have them.

[6] Congr. Globe, 2d Sess., 33d Congr., p. 729, statement of Mr. Clayton.

[7] *Ibid.*, 1st Sess., 35th Congr., p. 39.

adversely reported are generally postponed without debate.[3] Now the committees are the only machinery by which the senate investigates questions of law and fact,[2] and, as Mr. Voorhees said at the last session of congress "The final exercise of sovereign legislative power is ofttimes and to a large extent performed by committees."[3] Thus everything depends upon their formation and intelligent action.

In the appointment of other than the standing committees the rule has always been the same, that is, they have been appointed by ballot, a plurality of votes electing, except between 1823 and 1826 when they, as well as the standing committees, were appointed by the presiding officer.

Conference committees, by usage, always consist of three members on each side. At the head of the senate conferees is usually the man who has had charge of the bill in the senate. The rules provide for the appointment of these committees by ballot unless otherwise ordered. Generally the conference committee is left free, though there have been cases in which it was instructed.[4] In an ordinary free conference, to which bills are usually referred, the only limitation of the committee is that they shall not put in new matter which has not been proposed in either house.[5] The report of a conference committee is of a privileged character, and can be made at any

[1] Congr. Globe, 2d Sess., 35th Congr., p. 119. Also 1st Sess., 39th Congr., p. 3868, when in one evening nineteen adverse reports were made by a committee and accepted without debate.

[2] Congr. Record, 47th Congr., Special Sess., p. 15.

[3] The rule which allows a committee reporting a bill to amend it as it pleases before individual senators have a chance has been influential in increasing the power of committees.

[4] For example, Congr. Globe, 1st Sess., 38th Congr., p. 900, and Congr. Record, 1st Sess., 49th Congr., pp. 7617–7628.

[5] Congr. Record, 2d Sess., 48th Congr., p. 1468. In the first session of the 49th Congress (p. 308), a joint rule, regulating this, was passed by the senate.

time "except when the journal is being read, or a question of order, or a motion to adjourn is pending, or while the senate is dividing; and, when received, the question of proceeding to the consideration of the report, if raised, shall be immediately put, and shall be determined without debate." The extensive powers exercised by committees of conference at the present time is well known. This power is due mainly to the great amount of business to be transacted, and has grown with its growth. As early as the first session of the Thirty-sixth Congress, Mr. Trumbull said: "A practice has grown up here—abominable, I may say—by which the legitimate duty devolving upon the whole body is turned over to a committee of conference."[1] This state of affairs has become steadily more noticeable.

[1] Congr. Globe, p. 3028.

# CHAPTER III.

## THE SENATE AS A LEGISLATIVE BODY.

### I. SECRET SESSIONS OF THE SENATE.

WHEN the First Congress met at New York in the City Hall the senate chamber was a wainscoted room, about forty feet square and fifteen high.[1] The senators were seated in a semi-circle around the chair of the vice president, being arranged according to states, the senators from New Hampshire on the right of the president and those from Georgia on the left.[2] As the number of senators was so small, the transaction of business was comparatively easy, so that but few rules were needed, and this gave rise to practices which, though suitable and advantageous then, have become inconvenient and embarrassing now that the number of members is four times as great and the bulk of legislation vastly increased.

Much of the time of the senate during the first session of congress was necessarily occupied with its organization, and the decision of the questions as to

[1] *Pennsylvania Packet*, March 12, 1789.

[2] According to Rule I given by Mr. Maclay (Journal of Maclay, p. xiii). It is difficult to decide just what credence should be given to these rules of Mr. Maclay which were found written upon the cover of his journal, and which differ in many respects from those given in the senate journal. They are such as might be expected if a senator had attempted to write down from memory the rules of the senate, adding interpretations which they had received and practices which were followed though not embodied in the rules. They sometimes contain in one rule what in the senate journal is given as two, and *vice versa*. They also contain entirely new matter for which there is often no other authority and which in one case is certainly contrary to fact (Rule 9), and in two other cases probably is so (parts of rules 7 and 12).

mode of procedure, etc., which must come up at the establishment of a new government. The holding of its sessions with closed doors, which in the light of its future development was, perhaps, the most important step taken by the senate at this time, was provided for by no rule and seems to have been entered upon without debate and without question. At that time secret sessions of legislative bodies were not as uncommon as they now are, and consequently the action of the senate attracted less attention than it would now. Prior to 1766, when on the motion of James Otis the general court of Massachusetts yielded to the demand for publicity of debates, no legislative body of America had admitted the public to its sessions;[1] and the congress of the confederation and the convention for framing the constitution had both sat with closed doors.

Nothing is said upon the subject in the debates of the convention, but from a passage in the "Federalist" in which Hamilton draws a favorable comparison between the mode of appointment adopted by the constitution of the United States and that of New York, where the council of appointments confirmed nominations in secret, it would seem that open sessions were expected. On the other hand, if this were the case it is strange that the sessions should have been held in secret without any rule being made on the subject, and apparently without any question being raised. Even Washington did not know the reason which had led the senate to adopt this practice, but he suggests that it may have been to avoid speaking to the gallery, of which there was too much in the other house.[2]

The remonstrances which were shortly made against the secret sessions soon forced the senate to consider the

[1] Eaton, Secret Sessions, p. 12.

[2] Washington, Works, vol. XI, p. 411. Letter to David Stuart, July 26, 1789.

subject. In the second session of the First Congress Mr. Lee of Virginia, in obedience to his instructions, submitted a resolution for the opening of the doors of the senate and supported it by a speech occupying two days. No one replied and when the question was put Mr. Lee was supported by but two votes. Nevertheless the subject was brought up again and again. Jealousies of the senate began to arise in the minds of the people on account of its secret sessions.[1] It was urged that secret sessions destroyed the best security against mal-administration and annihilated the influence of the people over one branch of the government;[2] and, finally, in the first session of the Third Congress a motion for opening the doors when the senate was sitting in its legislative capacity, except in such cases as in the opinion of the senate required secrecy, was passed,[3] and at the next session the doors were opened to the public.

The debates, however, were still but little reported and, though the papers of the time generally contained daily accounts of the proceedings of the house when congress was in session, it is only rarely that those of the senate were referred to. A further advance towards publicity was made in 1802, when it was agreed to admit a stenographer to the floor of the senate.[1]

### II. QUORUM OF THE SENATE.

The first congress under the new constitution was slow in assembling and it seemed at first that the irregularity of attendance prevalent in the old congress was to reappear in the new. But eight senators were in their places on the fourth of March; and, in spite of two circular letters to the absent members, one of March the

[1] Annals of Congr., 3d Congr., 1st Sess., p. 34.

[2] Annals of Congr., 2d Sess., 2d Congr., pp. 625, 626; 1st Sess., 3d Congr., pp. 33, 34.

[3] *Ibid.*, 1st Sess., 3d Congr., p. 46.

[4] Sen. Journal, 1st Sess., 7th Congr., vol. III, pp. 165-166.

eleventh and the other a week later, a quorum was not secured until April sixth. Those who had appeared at the appointed time, full of interest and eager anticipation, felt no little chagrin at this apparent indifference. There were, however, excellent reasons for the delay. The New York senators had not yet been elected and others were detained by sickness, while, as Madison wrote to Jefferson, "The season of the year, the peculiar badness of the weather, and the short interval between the epoch of election, and that of meeting" formed a better apology for the delay than would be likely to occur to one on the other side of the Atlantic.[1] In succeeding sessions quorums were obtained with but little or no delay.

In order to keep a quorum after it was once obtained a rule was adopted providing that: "No member shall absent himself from the service of the Senate without leave of the Senate first obtained";[2] and, according to Mr. Maclay, violation of this rule was to be punished by writing on a slip of paper the name of the senator so doing, together with the nature of his transgression, and annexing it to the rules which hung in the senate chamber, there to remain until the senate, on his application or otherwise, should take action on the same.[3]

In the early days senators usually asked for leave of absence, and numerous entries regarding it are found in the journals;[4] occasionally, also, notices of senators absent without leave appear.[5] Gradually, however, the

[1] Madison, Works, I, p. 458. Letter of March 29, 1789.

[2] Annals of Congr., 1st Sess., 1st Congr., p. 21, Rule XIX.

[3] Journal of Maclay, p. xiv, Rule XVI.

[4] Benton says: "In the first age of the government, no member absented himself from the services of the House to which he belonged without first asking and obtaining its leave, or if called off suddenly, a colleague was engaged to state the circumstances to the House and ask the leave. (Thirty Years' View, II, 178, 179.)

[5] At the second session of the Fifth Congress a resolution was adopted two months before the end of the session, which provided "That the Secretary of the Senate be directed to write to all such

rule came to be disregarded. Benton says that he recollects "no instance of leave asked since the last of the early members, the Macons, Randolphs, Rufus Kings," etc.;[1] and by the Forty-seventh Congress the rule had so long been disregarded that when a senator asked for leave of absence a question was raised as to the necessity of his so doing, and the vice president stated that, though the rule was perfectly explicit, it had not been the practice of the senate to enforce it.[2]

Even while pretty carefully observed, the rule was found to be insufficient for the purpose of maintaining a quorum. Thus when such an important matter as the Jay treaty was before the senate it was with difficulty that a sufficient number of senators were kept together to decide it;[3] and in the second session of the Fifth Congress so many senators were absent, two months before the end of the session, that the secretary was directed to write to those absent without leave, requesting their immediate attendance.[4] The same session the rules were amended so as to authorize a number less than a quorum to send the sergeant-at-arms after any or all the absent members at the expense of the absentees, unless an excuse for non-attendance, deemed sufficient by the senate, were made.[5]

Attempts made under this rule to move the compulsory attendance of absentees were held out of order without a day's notice, and in 1877 the rules were changed

Senators as are absent without leave, or whose leave of absence has expired, requesting their immediate attendance." (Annals of Congr., p. 558.)

[1] Thirty Years' View, II. 178, 179.

[2] Congr. Record, 1st Sess., 47th Congr., p. 4401.

[3] Goodrich writes to Wolcott: "It has wounded us extremely that no remonstrances or respect for public business have been able to keep Senators and members of our House here a few days or a week." (Gibb's Administration of Washington and Adams, I. p. 343.)

[4] Annals of Congress, 2d Sess., 5th Congr., p. 558.

[5] Annals of Congress, 2d Sess., 5th Congr., p. 589, Rule 19.

so as to give to the senate the "power to request, and, when necessary, to compel the attendance of the absent Senators."[1]

Previously an attempt had been made to decrease the the number of absentees by the publication in the Congressional Globe of the names of those absent at every vote on which the yeas and nays were recorded. This rule, adopted in 1864,[2] was repealed in 1875,[3] but the names of those absent on every roll call have nevertheless still been published.

Attempts were also made to secure the attendance of senators by a deduction from their salary for absences. This was first tried in 1816, when provision was made for a deduction from the salary of all those absent either at the beginning or during the session of the senate, except in case of sickness.[4] This law, however, was repealed in 1817,[5] and the law passed in 1818 had little or no effect in restraining absences; for, though it provided that senators should receive pay only for days when they attended the senate, except when their absence was due to certain specified causes, these causes were so all embracing[6] as to make the restriction of little use, and its efficacy was sometimes still further diminished by the passage of a resolution at the end of the session providing that senators who did not take their seats at the opening of the session "by reason of sickness of themselves or families,

[1] Rule 3. Under this rule it was held necessary to first request the attendance of absent senators. (Congr. Record, 3d Sess., 45th Congr., p. 1847; 2d Sess., 51st Congr., p. 1437.)

[2] Congr. Globe, 1st Sess., 38th Congr., p. 2090.

[3] *Ibid.*, 2d Sess., 43d Congr., p. 1669.

[4] Statutes at Large, vol. 3, pp. 257, 258, 1st Sess., 14th Congr., chap. XXX.

[5] Statutes at Large, vol. 3, p. 345, 2d Sess., 14th Congr., chap. IX.

[6] Statutes at Large, vol. 3, p. 404, 1st Sess., 15th Congr., chap. V. The law provided that if a senator were detained by sickness on his journey or if he were unable to attend the senate after his arrival, he should nevertheless receive the regular *per diem* allowance.

providential causes or necessary business," should nevertheless receive the regular *per diem* allowance.[1]

The rule adopted in 1818 remained in force, though attempts were frequently made to change it, until 1856, when it was repealed, and a rule adopted which provided that a deduction from the salary of any senator should be made for every day's absence unless he should assign as a reason the sickness of himself or family.[2] In 1862, in order to keep senators at their places toward the end of the session, it was further provided that when a senator, in anticipation of the adjournment of the senate, withdrew from his seat without leave and did not return, he should forfeit, in addition to the sum deducted for each day's absence, an amount equal to the mileage allowed for his return home.[3] In 1866, when the law regarding salaries was again changed, no deduction for absences was provided for.

During most of the war the question of a quorum was of especial importance, for it had not then been decided whether the clause of the constitution which provides that "a Majority of each [house] shall constitute a Quorum",[4] meant a majority of all those who by any possibility might be elected, or only a majority of those who had been elected and were entitled to take their seats. If the former was held then, after the secession of the southern states, the absence for any reason of a very few senators would have been enough to break a quorum. The house had, at the first session of congress after the secession of the southern states, decided that a quorum of the house was a majority of those who had been elected and were entitled to take their seats. Precedents could be found in the practice of the senate in

[1] Congr. Globe, 1st Sess., 33d Congr., p. 2092.

[2] Statutes at Large, vol. 11, p. 48, 1st Sess., 34th Congr., chap. 123.

[3] Congr. Globe, 2d Sess., 37th Congr., pp. 3377–8.

[4] Art. I, sec. V.

support of each interpretation. At the first session of the First Congress, there being eleven states in the union, entitled to twenty-two senators, but the New York senators not yet having been elected, eleven were not considered a quorum. The next session, however, the opposite interpretation was given. There being twelve states, entitled to twenty-four senators, and one of the senators having recently died, twelve were considered a quorum. The next time, November sixth, 1804, under exactly similar circumstances the opposite was held, and in 1812 under similar circumstances this latter decision was adhered to;[1] but finally in 1864 a resolution was adopted declaring that a quorum of the senate consisted of a majority of the senators duly chosen.[2]

The difficulty in maintaining a quorum, due at first only to senators absenting themselves from attendance in the senate, has been increased in later times by the growth of two customs, unknown in the earlier days, namely, pairing off and refusing to vote, the object of the latter generally being to break a quorum.

The custom of pairing off was long in reaching the senate. Mr. Benton says that the first instance in the house of representatives when being "paired" was given as a reason for not voting was in 1840, and that, during the thirty years he was in the senate, he had never seen an instance of it; but, says he, "the practice has since penetrated that body; and 'pairing off' has become as common in that House as in the other. As a consequence, the two Houses are habitually found voting with deficient numbers—often to the extent of a third—often with a bare quorum."[3]

The pair usually extended only to political questions, so that a senator who was paired, and in the senate, could

[1] Congr. Globe, 2d Sess., 37th Congr., p. 3191, for list of cases.

[2] Congr. Globe, 1st Sess., 38th Congr., p. 2087.

[3] Benton, Thirty Years' View, II, p. 178.

vote on a non-political question or on a roll call. Consequently there might appear to be a quorum present at all times, except when the yeas and nays were demanded on a political question. The annoyance in keeping a quorum arising from this, recently led to a proposal to count, for the purposes of a quorum, all senators present and paired.[1]

The first rules adopted in the senate provided that every member present in the senate, when the yeas and nays were called, should vote, unless he were excused for special reasons;[2] and, under this rule, it was for some time the practice to allow senators to vote or not as they pleased, when a quorum was present.[3] Beginning with about 1850 efforts were occasionally made to compel senators to vote.[4] These attempts, however, were so few that in the Forty-sixth Congress it was stated that: "The practice of the Senate in permitting its members, without question, or challenge, to withhold their votes, whenever they have thought fit to do so, has been so uniform and unbroken, that, so far as precedents can make it so, it has become an absolute parliamentary right, and cannot be questioned without reversing the steady practice upon which the members of the body have a right to rely as their protection in the exercise of their discretion in giving or withholding their votes."[5] Ordinarily, when a senator refrained from voting, no notice would be taken of it; and it was only when attention was called to the fact by some one that the senate would have to

[1] Congr. Record, 1st Sess., 53d Congr., p. 2536.

[2] Rule XI.

[3] Statement of the vice president in 1851, Congr. Globe, 2d Sess., 31st Congr., p. 248.

[4] For example, in 1851, 2d Sess., 31st Congr., p. 248; also 3d Sess., 41st Congr., p. 1603, and 1st Sess., 46th Congr., p. 2147.

[5] Congr. Record, 3d Sess., 46th Congr., p. 2423.

vote whether or not to excuse the member.[1] There was, however, no provision for compelling a senator to vote if, after the senate had voted not to excuse him, he should still refuse to vote, and it has been repeatedly held that it could not be done.[2] A decision of the vice president in the first session of the Forty-sixth Congress, that on the question of excusing a senator from voting, a quorum must be present, made it impossible to obtain a quorum by refusing to excuse a senator from voting.[3] A ruling made at the same time to the effect that the fact of no quorum voting was not conclusive evidence that there was no quorum present, but that the chair had a right to count the senate to ascertain and, if he discovered a quorum present, business might be proceeded with,[4] greatly diminished the efficiency of this means of retarding business, by making it possible to proceed with debate, though not to a vote, should a quorum be present in the senate, even though a quorum was not voting.

A decision of the second session of the Fiftieth Congress,[5] that after a vote showing no quorum, and a roll call showing the presence of one, it was not in order to move the sergeant-at-arms to request the attendance of absent senators, made it impossible to bring to a decision any question on which the yeas and nays were demanded and for which a quorum was necessary, if senators, by remaining in the senate and yet refusing to vote,

[1] When this began to be done occasionally, questions arose as to the time at which attention should be called to the fact, etc. (Congr. Record, 2d Sess., 31st Congr., p, 248; 3d Sess., 41st Congr., p. 1603), which finally led to the adoption of a rule regulating it. (Rule 17, adopted in 1877.)

[2] 1st Sess., 46th Congr., 2147; 3d Sess., 46th Congr., 2423. In 1879 an unsuccessful attempt was made to compel a senator to vote by ordering the sergeant-at-arms to request his attendance. (1st Sess., 46th Congr., p. 2147.)

[3] Congr. Record, 1st Sess., 46th Congr., p. 2175.

[4] *Ibid.*, 2174, 2175.

[5] Congressional Record, 2d Sess., 50th Congress, p. 1043.

chose to break a quorum. The senate would, however, still be entitled to proceed with debate.[1] Proposals made providing that, when a quorum was present though not voting, senators present and not voting should be entered in the journal and counted for a quorum, and the vote announced accordingly[2], have not been brought to a vote.

If there be no call for the yeas and nays and no one calls attention to the lack of a quorum, business may go on indefinitely, and indeed much of the time now a quorum is not present in the senate. Especially is this the case when a debate is going on. The number of senators in the chamber scarcely averages twenty-five on such occasions, though if there is a roll call a sufficient number of senators to constitute a quorum will usually assemble from various portions of the capitol. In the early years, if the rule given by Mr. Maclay may be trusted, this was not the case, a withdrawal from the senate chamber for more than a quarter of an hour being punished in the same manner as neglect of attendance during a session.[3]

The absenting of themselves by senators in order to escape the responsibility of a vote is not a matter of recent occurrence, examples of it being found in very early times.

### III. ORDER OF PROCEDURE.

In the early congresses the regular hour of meeting seems to have been eleven A. M., and the length of the session ordinarily about four hours.[4] Now, however, for a long time, twelve o'clock has been the usual hour for assembling and the length of the session about five hours; but, as business becomes more pressing toward

[1] Congr. Record, 1st Sess., 51st Congr., p. 3468, statement of Mr. Hoar.

[2] *Ibid.*, 1st Sess., 51st Congr., p. 3704; 1st Sess., 53d Congr., p. 2641.

[3] Journal of Maclay, p. xiv, Rule XVI.

[4] Washington, Works, XI, p. 483, note. Mr. Maclay says that it was often not more than an hour.

the middle or end of a session, the hour is changed to eleven and, when more time still is needed, to ten; and it is sometimes, for a short time, even put as early as nine. The session is also lengthened at the other end by taking a recess and holding an evening session. Proposals for thus lengthening the session are almost always objected to by some on the ground that it leaves no time for committee work or the examination of bills; and the evening session often proves of no avail, through the inability to obtain a quorum, and is usually occupied by some one or two persons who wish to make speeches, no action of the senate being taken.

During the early part of the session the senate almost always adjourns over Saturday and sometimes Friday also, and even Thursday occasionally, this being more frequent in the early days of the senate. When more time is required, however, the senate meets every day of the week except Sunday, and sometimes at the end of the session even that day is not given to rest.

As is but natural, even in the early days when no more business came before the senate than it could conveniently transact, there was some little hurry at the end of the session. Mr. Maclay writes in his journal for March second, of the third session of the First Congress, that more business was hurried through the senate that day than in a month of former sessions; and of the next day he says: "The House seemed in a continual hurricane. Speaking would have been idle, for no one would or could hear. . . . . It was patching, piecing, altering and amending, and even originating new business. . . ." The senate met again at six o'clock. "Fourteen resolves were proposed and carried through," and then, according to Mr. Maclay, the confusion became so great that he was unable to tell what was being done.[1]

At the next session there was business enough to

[1] Journal of Maclay, 409-411.

require evening sessions on the last two days and, from that time on, the crowding of bills to the end of the session becomes more and more noticeable.

Sometimes bills would be introduced and passed through all their stages, under a suspension of the rules, in one day, but this was not often done, as the senate was usually fully occupied in considering bills already somewhat advanced and in action on conference reports and bills sent it from the other house.[1] As early as the Fourth Congress this press was felt sufficiently to lead to a proposal for a rule forbidding the origination of a law of general importance within the last ten days of the session, and declaring that the senate would act on none received from the house within that time.[2] The rule, however, was not adopted and the amount of business transacted on the last days of the session continued to increase. The editor of the Congressional Debates says in 1825: "Very little debate usually takes place within the last ten days of a Session, the time of both Houses being employed in perfecting business already matured by the committees, etc., . . . principally upon private bills, which seldom elicit more than a passing remark from the chairman of the committe which reported each bill, and sometimes not even that. We have known in the last week of the Session, as many as forty bills pass in one day;" but these pass without debate.[3]

Mr. Clay said that nearly all the business of the last session of the Twenty-fifth Congress was done in the last thirty days of the session;[4] and Mr. Hale, in the first session of the Thirty-fourth Congress, said that thirteen years of experience in the senate confirmed his idea that

[1] Bills were lost at every session for lack of time.

[2] Annals of Congr., 2d Sess., 4th Congr., pp. 1576, 1577.

[3] Congr. Debates, vol. I, 2d Sess., 18th Congr., pp. 741-742, note.

[4] Congr. Globe, 1st Sess., 26th Congr., p. 251.

all the business of the session, irrespective of its length, was done in the last two weeks of the senate,—a theory which would seem to be justified by the passage, in one morning, of fifty bills of which no one knew the subject except the senator who moved to take them up.[1] In the Sixteenth Congress seventy or eighty bills were signed between eight at night of the last day of the session and the next morning; and, on one occasion, seven laws passed their three readings in ten minutes.[2]

In order to prevent a repetition of this in the future, two rules were added by the Seventeenth Congress to the joint rules. The first provided that: "No bill that shall have passed one House shall be sent for concurrence to the other on either of the three last days of the session;" and the second that: "No bill or resolution that shall have passed the House of Representatives and the Senate shall be presented to the President of the United States, for his approbation, on the last day of the session."[3]

Had legislation been conducted in accordance with these rules there would certainly have been a considerable improvement; but, at almost every session thereafter, while the joint rules were in force, one or both of the rules would be suspended in favor of certain or all the bills of the session. Thus, of 142 bills passed in 1832–33, 90 were signed under suspension of the rules. At first it was held that these rules could be suspended whenever a majority wished, without a day's notice;[4] but, in 1836, it was held that it required unanimous consent to consider a resolution from the house suspending the rules on the same day that it was received.[5] In 1852

[1] Congr. Globe, 1st Sess., 33d Congr., p. 2214, statement of Mr. Pratt.

[2] Annals of Congress, 1st Sess., 17th Congr., p. 273.

[3] Annals of Congr., 1st Sess., 17th Congr., vol. I, p. 143.

[4] Congr. Deb., vol. VII, 2d Sess., 21st Congr., p. 334.

[5] *Ibid.*, vol. XII, part ii, 1st Sess., 24th Congr., p. 1937.

the rules were amended so as to provide that such a motion should "always be in order, be immediately considered and decided without debate."[1]

Thus matters remained until the Forty-fourth Congress, when it was decided in the senate that the joint rules did not hold over from one congress to the next, and a joint resolution accordingly passed re-adopting those of the previous session.[2] The house, however, seems to have thought differently; at least it did not adopt the resolution sent it by the senate, and, at the end of the session, sent up a resolution for the suspension of the joint rules. The senate refused to act upon this, sending to the house a resolution stating that, in their opinion, there were no joint rules.[3] Thus, since 1876, there has not even been the restraint of the sixteenth and seventeenth joint rules on the pushing of important business to the end of the session.[4]

To gain more time at the end of a session, the date of adjournment is frequently extended at those sessions whose termination is not fixed; and, in the latter case, a few hours are sometimes obtained by turning back or stopping the senate clock so that business can be done after midnight of March third, the time at which it seems at first to have been generally supposed that congress ended.[5]

At the second session of the Thirtieth Congress, when objections were made to the continuation of the session after twelve o'clock, the objections were overruled, and

[1] Congr. Globe, 1st Sess., 32d Congr., p. 1288, Rule 26.

[2] Congr. Record, 1st Sess., 44th Congr., p. 520.

[3] *Ibid.*, p. 5567.

[4] It would seem that the senate no longer wished to be restrained by these rules, for the joint rules which the senate has since adopted, but which have not been agreed to by the house, have contained no rules corresponding to the old 16th and 17th rules.

[5] Benton, Thirty Years' View, I, p. 555.

the session continued until 7 A. M. of March fourth ;[1] and, at the next congress, it was decided that the term of senators did not expire till noon of March fourth.[2]

The disorder which often prevailed in the senate, near its close, when there was much more business to be transacted than could possibly be got through with, and when everyone wished to secure the passage of his pet project, was often great. Mr. King, in taking the chair of the senate, March 3, 1841, said that: "He must be permitted to say that he had witnessed, on several occasions, at the close of the session of congress, a degree of excitement which did not, in his opinion, comport with the grave duties of the senate, and which was calculated to impair the weight of their deliberations, and was not calculated to facilitate the dispatch of their business . . . . if, unfortunately, there should be any departure from the strict order, he should feel it his duty to check it instantly."[3] The talking and confusion on the floor, which makes it difficult to get attention, and the scramble of six, eight, or ten senators for the floor, in more recent times, is notorious.

After the reading of the journal, it has always been the custom to devote a certain amount of time, usually an hour, to the despatching of matters for preparing and expediting business. At first there was no rule on the subject, but Jefferson in his "Parliamentary Manual"[4] says that such was the practice of the senate, and that no bills were put on their passage until twelve o'clock. A rule, adopted in 1834, which provided for the presentation of petitions and reports from standing committees after the reading of the journal, says nothing of the time

[1] Congr. Globe, 2d Sess., 30th Congr., pp. 686–692.

[2] *Ibid.*, 2d Sess., 31st Congr., p. 820.

[3] Congr. Globe, 2d Sess., 26th Congr., p. 225. A stronger statement on the same subject by Mr. Greeley may be found in Parton's Life of Greeley, p. 280.

[4] Section XIV.

which was to be so occupied; but it still seems to have been customary to devote an hour to such business.[1] In 1877 the morning hour was made a definite period; but in 1883 it was again made indefinite, provision being made for proceeding to the consideration of the general calendar, under the Anthony rule, immediately after the conclusion of the morning business, or at one o'clock, and continuation of it until two o'clock.[2]

At first new matter could be introduced at any time except when a question was before the house;[3] and it was not until 1868 that the rules provided for the introduction of bills during the morning hour.[4]

The first rules adopted provided for at least one day's notice of an intended motion for leave to introduce a bill.[5] The setting aside of this rule by unanimous consent in the case of nearly all bills, and the consequent encumbrance of the journal by the repetition of the words, "I ask leave to introduce a bill without having given previous notice," having become very general, a committee was appointed in 1874 to prepare an amendment to the rule, the restraint of which it was thought was sometimes needed. Various means of avoiding the inconvenience and yet maintaining the essential part of the rule were tried.[6] Finally, a rule was adopted which provided that: "Whenever a bill or joint resolution shall be offered, its introduction shall, if objected to, be postponed for one day."

The rules have always provided for three readings of all bills and resolutions and, prior to 1877, these readings

[1] Congr. Globe, 1st Sess., 35th Congr., p. 717, statement of the vice president.

[2] Rule VIII.

[3] Jefferson, Manual, sec. XIV.

[4] Rule 24.

[5] Rule 12.

[6] Congr. Record, 1st Sess., 44th Congr., p. 574; 2d Sess., 44th Congr., p. 627.

had to be on separate days, unless otherwise ordered by the unanimous consent of the senate. It was then provided[1] that bills and joint resolutions from the house of representatives or from a committee could be read twice on the same day, if not objected to.

By 1843 it had come to be the practice for all three readings of the bill to be by title only; and, attention being called to it, the vice president decided that the rules of the senate required the reading of bills through on their second reading; whereupon it was done for a few days, but was found to consume so much time that the one who, in the first place, had objected to the practice, said that: "He hoped it would be the understanding in the future, that all bills would be read the first and second times, before reference to a committee, by their titles only, unless any senator should call for the reading entire of particular bills." This was accordingly done.[2]

The first rule adopted regarding the order of procedure after the conclusion of the morning business was that of 1820, which provided that the unfinished business of the last preceding session should have the precedence.[3] After this came the special orders, if any, and then the general orders.[4]

In 1858 a question was raised as to whether a special order, which had been made for a special time, if not finished on that day, came up the next day at the time for which it had been fixed at the previous day, or at one o'clock, and the latter was decided.[5]

When the amount of business became much greater the special orders, which were frequently made merely from courtesy to accommodate a senator, were found to

[1] Rule 24.

[2] Congr. Globe, 1st Sess., 28th Congr., p. 41.

[3] Rule 15.

[4] This was first embodied in the rules in 1870. (Congr. Globe, 2d Sess., 41st Congr., p. 1819.)

[5] Congr. Globe, 1st Sess., 35th Congr., p. 717.

be a hindrance to business; and in 1862 it was agreed, without opposition or debate, that thereafter a two-thirds vote should be required to make any subject a special order.[1] As the end of the session approaches, in later days, a special time has often been set aside for the consideration of special classes of bills; and these special orders have sometimes become so numerous as to leave little time for the transaction of the regular business, and made it necessary to rescind all such orders.[2]

Occasionally a whole session has been set aside for the consideration of a special subject. Mr. Clay wished so to limit the business of the special session of the Twenty-seventh Congress, but the resolution introduced by him for this purpose was not acted upon, and it was not until the adjourned session of the Fortieth Congress, which met July 3, 1867, that such a limitation was adopted. It was then decided to confine the business of the session to removing obstructions to the acts of reconstruction and giving them the scope intended. The decision was not reached without strong objections being made to it, notably by Mr. Sumner, who declared it unconstitutional.[3] A similar resolution was adopted at the first session of the Forty-second Congress and at the first session of the Forty-sixth Congress.

The course of a private bill in the senate is generally the same as that of a public bill. Though there is no time set aside by the standing rules for their consideration, as there is in the house, special days are frequently ordered to be devoted to their consideration for the remainder of the session, or until they are disposed of.

[1] Congr. Globe, 2d Sess., 37th Congr., pp. 287, 288. This has since been the rule on the subject.

[2] Congr. Globe, 2d Sess., 41st Congr., p. 1819; Congr. Globe, 2d Sess., 46th Congr., p. 1403.

[3] Congr. Globe, 1st Sess., 40th Congr., pp. 481–498.

Recently some restrictions have been placed upon the repeated re-introduction of claims once rejected by congress. The senate passed a joint resolution for this purpose at two succeeding sessions of the Twenty-seventh Congress, but the resolution was not considered by the house; and there seems to have been no restriction of this sort until long after, when a senate rule was adopted,[1] forbidding bringing up a claim on which an adverse report had been made and accepted, unless new evidence had been discovered. As it is not very difficult to obtain new evidence, this has not proved much of a restraint.[2]

The increasing number of private bills, which occupied so much of the time of the senate, led, in 1856, to the adoption of a rule providing that: "Whenever a private bill is under consideration, it shall be in order to move as a substitute for it, a resolution of the senate referring the case to the Court of Claims." This rule seems to have been dropped some time between 1868 and 1877, but in 1883[3] a rule authorizing the reference to the court of claims of all claims involving the determination of facts, was adopted in accordance with a statute of that year.[4]

A practice had grown up in the senate of securing the passage of private bills, which had failed on their merits, or for the consideration of which a time could not be found, by tacking them to the appropriation bills. To prevent this, a rule was adopted in 1850, which declared that no amendment, providing for a private claim, should be received, even though the same had been previously sanctioned by the senate.[5] This was soon amended by striking out that part of the rule which reads "although

[1] No. 58 of the rules adopted in 1877, and No. 31 of the present rules.

[2] Congr. Record, 1st Sess., 48th Congr., p. 1078.

[3] Rule XVI, sec. 3. Now found in Rule XV, sec. 3.

[4] Statutes at Large, vol. 22, p. 485, 2d Sess., 47th Congr., chap. 116.

[5] Congr. Globe, 2d Sess., 31st Congr., p. 78.

the same may have been previously sanctioned by the senate," and inserting "unless it be to carry out the provisions of an existing law, or a treaty stipulation."[1]

In recent times the number of private bills has increased so much as to occupy an undue amount of the time of the senate, and this has led to numerous proposals for rules restricting the introduction of such bills.[2]

According to the usage of the British parliament, unfinished business of one session was destroyed by a dissolution or prorogation of parliament; and, soon after the organization of the new government, a joint committee of the two houses decided that such was the proper mode of procedure to be followed by congress.[3] All attempts made to change this decision failed, until 1848, when a joint resolution was adopted providing that all "bills, resolutions, or reports" of either house, undetermined at one session, should be resumed and acted upon "after six days from the commencement of a second or subsequent session of Congress."[4] A question arising in the senate as to whether this included petitions, a resolution was adopted in 1854 providing that all business undetermined at one congress should be resumed at the next, no time for so doing being mentioned. The question raised at subsequent sessions as to whether or not this rescinded the joint rule was not decided.[5] A similar resolution was adopted at succeeding sessions and was added to the standing rules in 1868,[6] the member of the committee who reported the rules declaring that the committee did not consider that the rule repealed the joint rule, but that it was in harmony with it.[7] At the same

[1] Congr, Globe., 1st Sess., 33d Congr., p. 1058.

[2] For example, Congr. Record, 1st Sess., 48th Congr., p. 1077.

[3] Sen. Journal, vol. I, 2d Sess., 1st Congr., p. 107.

[4] Congr. Globe, 1st Sess., 30th Congr., p. 1085.

[5] *Ibid.*, 3d Sess., 42d Congr., p. 2.

[6] Rule 52.

[7] Congr. Globe, 3d Sess., 41st Congr., p. 4, Mr. Edmunds.

time a question was raised as to whether the joint rules forbade action before six days had elapsed. The house had held that it did not, but the senate that it did;[1] but as the joint rules ceased to exist soon after this, there is no longer this restriction on the action of the senate.

Executive business has ordinarily been taken up at the end of the day's session, unless there was something that could not wait, or would require an entire day.

### IV. LIMITATIONS OF DEBATE.

In the early days of the senate, debate was practically unlimited, the restraints placed upon it being slight and seldom enforced. They were, that no motion should be debated until seconded, that the decision of all questions of order should be made by the president without debate, and that no member should speak more than twice in any one debate on the same day without leave of the senate. The previous question, which was provided for by the rules[2] but rarely used,[3] and was omitted in the revision of the rules in 1806, was not used to limit debate, but as in the continental congress and the parliament of England, where the previous question was used to avoid a vote on a given subject. The proper occasion for its use was, according to Mr. Jefferson, to get rid of subjects "of a delicate nature as to high personages, etc., or the discussion of which may call forth observa-

[1] *Ibid.*, 2d Sess., 34th Congr., p. 1; 3d Sess., 41st Congr., pp. 3, 19; 3d Sess., 42d Congr., p. 2.

[2] Rule IX. "The previous question being moved and seconded the question from the chair shall be 'Shall the main question be now put?' And if the nays prevail, the main question shall not then be put." In the continental congress the usual form of the question was "Shall the main question be *not* now put?" and if decided in the affirmative the main question was not then put. In two instances this is the form used in the senate. (Exec. Jour., I, 96, 97.)

[3] Exec. Jour., I, pp. 96, 97, 318. Sen. Jour., 1st Sess., 1st Congr., pp. 60, 61. Annals of Congr., 1st Sess., 8th Congr., p. 363.

tions which might be of injurious consequences."[1] He, however, says that its use had been extended abusively to other cases; and by reference to the cases in which it was used in the senate, it would seem probable that its use there was, as in England at the present time, to enable the body to dispose of the subject without a direct vote upon it. The previous question was debatable[2] and was used in both legislative and executive session and in the trial of impeachments, but not on amendments,[3] or in the committee of the whole.[4]

In 1806, debate upon a motion for adjournment was forbidden,[5] and the following year debate on an amendment at the third reading of a bill;[6] but for many years thereafter no further limitations were imposed, and this freedom of debate was rarely abused.[7] Mr. Calhoun said, in 1840, that: "There never had been a body in this or any other country in which, for such a length of time, so much dignity and decorum of debate had been maintained."[8] These remarks were called forth by a proposal of Mr. Clay for the introduction of the previous question,[9] which, he stated, was rendered necessary by the abuse which the minority had made of the unlimited

[1] Manual, sec. XXXIV.

[2] *Ibid.*, sec. XXXIV. "Then the previous question is proposed and, in the modern usage, the discussion of the main question is suspended and the debate confined to the previous question." Maclay gives as a rule of the senate the following: "In case of a debate becoming tedious, four senators may call for the question, or the same number may at any time move for the previous question, viz: 'Shall the main question be now put?'" (Rule 7.) I can find no confirmation of this rule.

[3] Sen. Jour., vol. III, 1st Sess., 6th Congr., p. 27.

[4] Jefferson's Manual, sec. XXIV.

[5] Rule 8.

[6] Sen. Jour., vol. IV, 2d Sess., 9th Congr., pp. 135, 138, 139.

[7] See Benton on the subject, Congr. Globe, 1st Sess., 27th Congr., p. 204.

[8] Congr. Globe, 1st Sess., 27th Congr., p. 205.

[9] *Ibid.*, p. 203.

privilege of debate. The proposition met with so much opposition that it was abandoned; but the accusation of factious opposition on the part of the minority, made at that time,[1] was heard again and again in succeeding congresses; and this, together with the increasing amount of business to be transacted, which made some limitation of even legitimate debate seem desirable at times, led in the following years to several proposals having this object in view.[2] None, however, were adopted until the civil war, when it was agreed that, in the consideration in secret session of subjects relating to the rebellion, debate should be confined to the subject-matter and limited to five minutes, "except that five minutes be allowed any member to explain or oppose a pertinent amendment."[3] All other proposed limitations of debate failed[4] until 1868, when a rule was adopted providing that: "Motions to take up or to proceed to the consideration of any question, shall be determined without debate, upon the merits of the question proposed to be considered;" the object of the rule being, according to Mr. Edmunds, to prevent a practice which had grown up in the senate, "when a question was pending, and a senator wished to deliver a speech on some other question, to move to postpone the pending order and take up another; and then proceed to deliver their speech on the other question."[5] According

[1] Congr. Globe, 1st Sess., 27th Congr., p. 203.

[2] These were for a rule allowing an amendment to be laid on the table without the bill (Congr. Globe, 1st Sess., 31st Congr., p. 1688, and 1st Sess., 32d Cong., p. 1609), for the introduction of the previous question (Congr. Globe, 1st Sess., 31st Congr., pp. 1466, 1688), and for the limitation of debate, during the remainder of the session, to five minutes, except on leave granted (1st Sess., 35th Congr., p. 2526).

[3] Congr. Globe, 2d Sess., 37th Congr., pp. 490, 536.

[4] The limitations proposed were to allow a majority (Congr. Globe, 2d Sess., 37th Congr., p. 1557), or two-thirds (2d Sess., 41st Congr., pp. 1819, 2212), to fix the time for ending debate, and to allow amendments to appropriation bills to be laid upon the table without the bill (Congr. Globe, 2d Sess., 41st Congr., p. 4128).

[5] Congr. Globe, 2d Sess., 41st Congr., p. 508.

to Mr. Trumbull, the object of the rule was to prevent the consumption of time in debate over business to be taken up.[1] The rule was interpreted as preventing debate on the merits of a question when a proposal to postpone it was made.

As appropriation bills generally excited so much interest and discussion, it was natural that the necessity for limiting debate on them should be felt more than on other bills; and, about this time, many motions were made having this in view. The first to be agreed to was one allowing amendments to appropriation bills to be laid on the table without prejudice to the bill.[2] The efficacy of the rule, which had been repeatedly proposed and rejected, was soon acknowledged by all, and it was afterwards extended so as to apply to other bills as well.[3]

In the consideration of appropriation bills at the end of the session, in order to expedite business debate had, on several occasions, by unanimous consent, been confined to five minutes; and finally, in 1872, it was ordered that, during the remainder of the session, it should be in order, in the consideration of appropriation bills, to move to confine debate by any senator on the pending motion to five minutes.[4] The necessity for some limitation of debate caused the adoption of similar resolutions at most of the succeeding sessions.

The so-called Anthony rule which, for the expedition of business is the most important limitation of debate yet adopted, places no restraint upon the rights of the minority, inasmuch as a single objection will prevent its application to the subject under consideration. It was first adopted in the third session of the Forty-first Congress, when the great increase in the amount of busi-

[1] Congr. Globe, 2d Sess., 41st Congr., pp. 507, 508.

[2] *Ibid.*, 3d Sess., 41st Congr., p. 1477.

[3] Congr. Record, 1st Sess., 47th Congr., p. 1907.

[4] Congr. Globe, 2d Sess., 42d Congr., pp. 2867–2883, yeas 33, nays 13.

ness, which made it impossible to reach everything, and caused such a scramble for precedence that hours were often consumed in deciding what should be done, made it necessary to find some means of relief. The rule as first adopted provided that: "On Monday next, at one o'clock, the Senate will proceed to the consideration of the Calendar, and bills that are not objected to shall be taken up in their order; and each Senator shall be entitled to speak once and for five minutes, only, on each question; and this order shall be enforced daily at one o'clock till the end of the Calendar is reached, unless upon motion the Senate should at any time otherwise order."[1]

This regulation proving efficacious was adopted in succeeding sessions;[2] and finally, in the second session of the Forty-sixth Congress, was added to the standing rules. The vice president at the next congress having decided that, if a majority decided to take up a bill, on objection being made to its consideration, the limitation of debate would still apply, the rule was amended so as to prevent this.[3] When the regular morning hour is not found sufficient for the consideration of all unobjected cases on the calendar, special times are often set aside for the consideration of the calendar under the Anthony rule.

A proposal to require the objection of five to pass over a bill was at once objected to as a form of the previous question,[4] and all other proposals for a limitation of debate, which would also limit the power of the minority, have been repeatedly rejected; and, at present, there

[1] Congr. Globe, 3d Sess., 41st Congr., p. 28. The rule was interpreted as allowing objection to be made at any time. (Congr. Record, 2d Sess., 40th Congr., pp. 1302–1304.)

[2] I have found no notice of the adoption of this rule from this time until the second session of the Forty-fifth Congress, but when it was then proposed it was said that it had been used for some time.

[3] Congr. Record, 1st Sess., 47th Congr., p. 3345.

[4] *Ibid.*, 3d Sess., 46th Congr., p. 1693.

seems to be no probability of such a rule being adopted.

Though the senate has steadily refused to place general limitations on its right of debate, it is comparatively easy, when the question under consideration does not involve strong feeling, to secure unanimous consent to the limitation of debate to five or ten minutes, on the subject before the house. Similarly the time for ending debate and taking the vote is often fixed by unanimous consent.[1] The custom is first seen coming in at the Twenty-ninth Congress, when an unsuccessful attempt was made to induce the minority to fix a day for taking the vote on the Oregon Bill, which had been debated two months.

Usually, when there is no factious opposition, and the majority have been willing to grant to the minority a reasonable time for debate, there has been no difficulty in securing such unanimous consent. It has come to be the custom to thus fix the time for taking the vote on all the revenue bills,[2] and this practice doubtless contributes much to the rapidity with which the senate can transact business.

All the rules for the limitation of debate which have been adopted are such as were needed to restrain perfectly legitimate debate; and, as has been clearly proven of late, are little or no restraint upon the minority, should it wish to attempt factious opposition.

In the early days of congress no complaint is heard of factious opposition or dilatory motions, but from about 1850 such complaints begin to be heard.[3] The first in-

[1] Such an agreement was not enforced by the chair, but every senator felt bound to stand by it (Congr. Globe, 2d Sess., 41st Congr., p. 478; Congr. Record, 1st Sess., 51st Congr., p. 4129), and, according to senatorial usage, a number less than a quorum could make the agreement. (Congr. Globe, 3d Sess., 41st Congr., p. 1589, statement of vice president.)

[2] Congr. Record, 1st Sess., 51st Congr., p. 9109, statement of Mr. Gorman.

[3] For example, Congr. Globe, 1st Sess., 32d Congr., p. 1606; 1st Sess., 34th Congr., p. 1723; 3d Sess., 37th Congr., p. 1491.

stance in which the minority openly declared their intention of filibustering was in 1849, when Clay brought forward his proposition for a previous question; but, as the subject was not pushed, the minority were not forced to carry out their threats.

The right of the minority, under certain circumstances, to prevent action by all dilatory motions in their power, was avowed in 1879, when an attempt was made to repeal the then existing election laws, on an army appropriation bill, and the opposition of the minority forced the dropping of the measure. But the most notable case, prior to the recent one, happened at the special session of the Forty-seventh Congress, when the Republicans, having just obtained a majority in the senate, wished to change certain of the officers of the senate at the special session. The Democrats objected to the change being made at that time, and delayed action by long speeches, by motions to adjourn and to go into executive session, and by refusing to vote and so breaking a quorum. The struggle finally became one to decide whether the majority or minority should rule the senate. There were an equal number of Republican and Democratic senators so that the casting vote of the vice president was needed to make a majority for the Republicans. His right to a casting vote in the election of officers was questioned, and, on this ground, some of the minority, while acknowledging the right of the majority to govern as a rule, denied it in the present instance. This position, however, was invalidated by the refusal of one of the Democratic senators to vote with his party on this point, the vote of the vice president being, therefore, unnecessary for securing the action desired by the majority.[1]

The struggle, which began on the twenty-fourth of March, continued, almost without interruption, till May fourth, when a motion was made to go into executive

[1] Congr. Record, Special Sess., 47th Congr., p. 407.

session, the majority, however, declaring that they did not give up the struggle.[1] The subject was again brought up on the sixth and eleventh of May, but meeting with the same opposition was dropped, the minority thus coming off victorious. The debates in the senate and the articles in the newspapers were of much the same character as those seen during the recent contest between the majority and the minority in the senate, and the feeling excited against the senate was very considerable. The action of the minority in this case was less defensible than in the recent struggle, in that they could not then intrench themselves behind the assertion that they were resisting for the good of the country, as what was concerned was purely a party measure.

From this time on the minority have shown a disposition to make use of dilatory tactics to prevent any action of the majority to which they objected. In the second session of the Fifty-first Congress, the Democrats, being in but a small minority, attempted to dictate the order of business which should be followed. About forty-six days had been given to the debate on the Force Bill in the senate and, the minority still refusing to allow a vote to be taken, the majority then attempted to pass a resolution for the close of debate by the majority after a reasonable time, but this met with the most determined opposition. A session of four days without adjournment was held, at the end of which time the Republican majority gave way and moved to take up the apportionment bill. It was this action of the minority that led to the proposals for a limitation of debate which were so strongly urged during that session.

The recent action of the minority in the first session of the Fifty-third Congress, when the bill for the repeal of the purchasing clause of the Sherman act was discussed in the senate from August twenty-ninth to Oc-

[1] Congr. Record, 47th Congr., Special Session, p. 453.

tober thirty-first, on which day the minority gave way and allowed a vote to be taken, has raised in the minds of the people a very general contempt for that body, and numerous are the expressions to the effect that such a thing had never before happened in the senate. This feeling seems, however, to be but a repetition of that aroused against the senate at the special session of the Forty-seventh Congress, and scarcely stronger.

If the length of time occupied in the discussion is alone considered, it is seen that it was not much greater than has often been consumed in the discussion of important questions, on which opposing views were held, or which involved party questions. The difference between this discussion and that over the re-charter of the United States bank, for instance, lay in the open avowal, on the part of the minority, of their constitutional right to obstruct legislation by all means in their power, and their intention of using them; and in that all attempts of the majority, after reasonable time had been allowed for debate, to have a time, however distant, fixed for taking the vote, were unsuccessful, a night session failing to secure the desired end. All means of opposition were tried. Speeches which occupied three and four days were delivered. Senators refused to vote to make a quorum, and one dilatory motion after another was made. Attempts to change the rules were, of course, without avail. The vice president did not see fit to adopt the suggestion, frequently made, that he should refuse to recognize the members of the minority, nor was the suggestion of Judge Cooley, who held the action of the minority to be antagonistic to the constitution, adopted. He wrote: "Members of the majority should make the proper motions looking to definite and final action on the pending measure, and the presiding officer should recognize them; since only in that way can the inalienable right of the Senate to express its will be exercised."

This not being done, and the minority finally giving way, the rights of majorities and minorities have received no authoritative interpretation; and there seems, at present, no probability that a change of rules, even, will result from the action of the minority, much less a radical change in the constitution of the senate itself.

All other means of securing a vote on a given question having failed, an all-night session is usually tried. This was first found necessary in 1837, in order to secure a vote on the expunging from the journals of the resolution censuring President Jackson.[1] It was again tried in the first session of the Thirtieth Congress,[2] the session lasting till 8 A. M., before the vote was taken. As time went on and the difficulties of obtaining a vote on any subject increased, the number of all-night sessions became greater. They did not always succeed in their object, by any means. In the second session of the Thirty-ninth Congress, Mr. Wilson said that, in the twelve years he had been in the senate, he had never known anything to be gained by the policy of night sessions.[3] Frequently, however, a vote was obtained by this means and all-night sessions continued to be tried, almost every congress witnessing at least one such attempt.

On such occasions it is usual to give all the time for speaking to the minority. When night sessions were first used, the time seems to have been really occupied with debate, but later dilatory motions came to occupy most of the time. Often senators would refuse to vote so that it would be impossible to secure a quorum.

### V. APPROPRIATION BILLS.

The constitution provides that "All bills for raising Revenue shall originate in the House of Representatives;

[1] Benton, Thirty Years' View, I, pp. 727-731.

[2] Congr. Globe, pp. 999, 1002.

[3] Congr. Globe, p. 1396.

but the Senate may propose or concur with Amendments as on other Bills."[1] This clause has been the subject of much discussion, the phrase "All bills for raising Revenue" being interpreted, on the one hand, as preventing the senate from originating any bills for appropriating money, as well as for raising it; and, on the other, as laying a prohibition only upon the origination of bills for raising money. In support of the first view the use of the phrase "revenue bills," especially in England at the time of the adoption of the constitution, was cited, while the other side relied on the ordinary meaning of the word. Both sides appealed to the debates in the convention, attention being called on the one hand to the use of "money bills" and "revenue bills" as synonymous terms, and on the other to the fact that the clause as first reported read "All Bills for raising and appropriating money and for fixing the salaries," but as finally adopted read "All bills for raising Revenue."[2]

In support of the first view is the almost unbroken practice of the origination of the general appropriation bills in the house; but, on the other hand, there are numerous cases in which the senate has, without being questioned by the house, originated bills for all kinds of special appropriations.[3] Moreover the right of the senate to originate the general appropriation bills has been asserted by that house on several occasions. A resolution which indirectly declared the senate to have this power was introduced in 1797, but was postponed.[4] In 1816, however, a bill making additional appropriations

[1] Article I, sec. VII.

[2] Elliot, Debates, V, p. 377, Art. IV, sec. 5, as reported by the committee of detail.

[3] The instances of special appropriations originated in the senate are too numerous to be mentioned. The majority report of the judiciary committee in 1881 said that they would fill a volume. (3d Sess., 46th Congr., House Reports, No. 147, p. 10.)

[4] Sen. Jour., 2d Sess., 4th Congr., vol. II, p. 348.

for the year was not only introduced and passed in the senate,[1] but agreed to in the house without any objection being made to the place of origination.

In the first session of the Thirty-second Congress the senate, by implication, declared that it could originate appropriation bills by refusing to add "to the Senate" to a proposed rule which provided that: "All general appropriations shall be sent at least ten days previous to the day fixed for the adjournment of Congress."[2]

A few years later, the delay of the house in sending the appropriation bills caused the senate to instruct the committee of finance to "prepare and report such of the general appropriation bills as they may deem expedient." It was thus left indefinite, that they might confer with the committee of ways and means of the house and decide upon a division of the work.[3] Only one of the appropriation bills was introduced and passed in the senate, and this was not considered by the house, which introduced and passed a bill of its own that was accepted by the senate. Shortly after this, however, the house impliedly denied that appropriation bills were revenue bills, by denying the right of the senate to amend, by raising the rates of postage, a bill making appropriations for the post-office;[4] and at the third session of the Forty-sixth Congress the house committee on the judiciary, to whom the subject had been referred, upheld the right of the senate to originate all appropriation bills.[5]

Of late years the senate has not pushed its claims. A proposal at the first session of the Forty-seventh Congress to instruct the committee on appropriations to introduce the general appropriation bills, was not received with

[1] Sen. Jour., 1st Sess., 14th Congr., pp. 440, 632.

[2] Congr. Globe, 1st Sess., 32d Congr., p. 1787.

[3] *Ibid.*, 1st Sess., 34th Congr., pp. 160–163, 375–381.

[4] *Ibid.*, 2d Sess., 35th Congr., p. 1634.

[5] House Reports, No. 147.

favor;[1] and though at the second session of the Forty-eighth Congress the river and harbor bill was introduced in the senate, it was not, as was stated, with the object of raising the old question of the right of the senate to introduce the appropriation bills, but only to give the senate committee ample time for its consideration. The bill was that of the house with certain parts, disliked by the senate, stricken out; and, after its reference to the committee, no further action was taken by the senate. This attitude of the senate should not, however, be interpreted as a sign of weakness or submission to the house. The senate no longer claims the right of originating appropriations, because the right has ceased to be of any practical importance, being a disadvantage rather than an advantage, since, under the present system, the senate makes very radical changes in the appropriation bills which the house has, ordinarily, no time to consider or amend. Mr. Hoar, writing in 1879, held that the exclusive right of the house to originate money bills, gave to the senate a considerable preponderance of influence,[2] and its influence since then has rather increased than diminished.

Another point on which the senate and house have disagreed is as to whether or not a bill for reducing revenue is a bill for the raising of revenue. During the first half of the century leave was repeatedly granted in the senate for the introduction of bills reducing the revenue by diminishing duties or for the entire repeal of acts imposing duties; and many examples may be found of bills so originated having become laws.[3]

In 1833 the introduction in the senate of Clay's tariff compromise, was objected to because, though reduc-

[1] Congr. Record, pp. 4508, 4509.

[2] *North American Review*, vol. 128, p. 117.

[3] 3d Sess., 41st Congr., Sen. Reports, No. 376, p. 7.

ing the revenue in general, it contained one clause raising it;[1] and, though the objection was overruled in the senate and the bill introduced there, in order to avoid collision with the house an exactly similar bill, introduced and passed in the house, was, when received in the senate, made the basis of action there.[2] In 1844, however, leave was refused in the senate to revive this act on the same ground that objection had earlier been made to the introduction of the original bill.

The senate still maintained that it could introduce bills to reduce or entirely repeal duties, and laws of this character were agreed to by the house when introduced in the senate;[3] but in 1871 the house denied this right also.[4] The position taken by the house was so determined that, at the next congress, leave to introduce a bill for the reduction of the internal taxes was refused by the senate on the ground that it was useless, since the house would surely reject such a bill;[5] and, later, the senate committee on the judiciary reported against the right of the senate to introduce a bill for the reduction of taxation, though still maintaining that it could introduce one for the entire repeal of a law imposing taxes.[6]

The house, during the same session, in its eagerness to restrain the senate, indirectly reversed the decision of the previous session, and held a bill for repealing duties not a revenue bill, by declaring that the senate had no right to amend a bill of that character, then under consideration, so as to raise revenue.

At first all the general appropriation bills were made in one act, but in 1794 the army appropriation was made separately, and in 1798 the appropriation for the navy.

[1] Similar bills had earlier been introduced in the senate.

[2] Congr. Globe, 1st Sess., 28th Congr., pp. 159 ff., 165, 166, 633.

[3] 3d Sess., 41st Congr., Sen. Reports, No. 376, p. 7.

[4] 3d Sess., 41st Congr., Sen. Reports, No. 376.

[5] Congr. Globe, 2d Sess., 42d Congr., pp. 46, 47.

[6] 2d Sess., 42d Congr., Sen. Reports, No. 146.

In 1837 the general appropriation bills were "civil and diplomatic, army, navy, indian."[1] The appropriations for the several branches of the public service are now made in thirteen bills.[2] In the senate these are all referred to the committee on appropriations, though numerous attempts have been made to secure the reference of each of the appropriation bills to the committees having charge of the subject with which each bill is concerned.

For the first few congresses the appropriation bills were received from the house in good season, but in the first session of the Fourth Congress, an additional appropriation bill being necessary, it was introduced and rushed through the senate in the last two days of the session; and, at the next session, the bill making appropriations for the military and naval expenses was not received in the senate till March third. Unanimous consent to its immediate consideration was at first refused but later granted. At the same time a resolution was submitted, condemning the withholding of the appropriation bills till the end of the session as an infringement on the rights of the senate, and proposing the adoption of a rule forbidding the origination or receipt of such bills within the last ten days of the session.[3]

Though there was an improvement the next session, it did not last, and the practice in this regard became worse rather than better. The rule adopted in the house in 1837, requiring the committee on appropriations, within thirty days after the opening of the session, to report the general appropriation bills, or in failure thereof the reasons of such failure, seems to have had little effect;[4] and, the appropriation bills coming to the senate later and

[1] Rules of the House of Rep., 1st Sess., 45th Congr., p. 120.

[2] Rules of the House of Rep., 1st Sess., 51st Congr., pp. 287, 288.

[3] Annals of Congress, 2d Sess., 4th Congr., p. 1576.

[4] A list, giving the dates of the receipt of the appropriation bills, is given in Congr. Globe, 1st Sess., 34th Congr., pp. 160–161, and Congr. Record, 1st Sess., 49th Congr., p. 6373.

later, the senate in 1852 amended the sixteenth joint rule so as to provide that all appropriation bills should be sent at least ten days before the end of the session,[1] but the house failed to agree to the change. A proposal, made quite recently, for a rule forbidding a committee to report an appropriation bill within five days after its receipt, had in view the same object.

The impossibility of properly considering the bills in the short time usually left the senate, led at times, as has been seen, to the introduction of the bills in the senate; but, as there were such serious objections to this course on the ground of its unconstitutionality, it has not often been tried. It is, however, perfectly possible for the senate committees to consider bills before their receipt from the house, and this is often done,[2] and it sometimes happens that amendments are offered by senators to appropriation bills before their receipt from the house.[3]

This custom, by which the senate can gain more time for the consideration of bills, added to the fact that the amendments which an appropriation bill now receives in the senate are most considerable, sometimes even an entirely new bill being substituted, has turned the tables so that now the house suffers more than the senate from the delay of the appropriation bills. For, frequently, when a bill is returned to the house, it is so late that there is no time to consider the amendments made by the senate, so that the house simply non-concurs in them, and the bill goes to a conference committee. There part of the senate amendments are put back on the bill, and, as the conference report is often adopted by the house without consideration, the amendments made by the senate are

[1] Congr. Globe, vol. 24, part III, 1st Sess., 32d Congr., p. 1787.

[2] It was done as early as the first session of the 32d Congress. (Congr. Globe, p. 1786.)

[3] For example, House Bill, No. 13,462, was not received in the senate until February 3, 1891, but on January 13, 1891, an amendment to it was proposed in the senate.

never considered by the house. Moreover, the wishes of the senate, when there is a difference of opinion upon a proposition originated in the senate, are much more apt to prevail when tacked to a bill to which the house has already given its assent, than when introduced as a separate bill. The fact that the senate is a more permanent body than the house also gives it an advantage every two years, in that the house knows that, if the senate insists on its amendments, and the bill is lost, the then existing house of representatives loses all power over the subject, as, at the extra session which is thus made necessary, its successors will have charge of the matter.

The house rule adopted in 1837, requiring all appropriation bills to be reported within thirty days after the beginning of congress or the reasons for not doing so, was retained as late as the Forty-fifth Congress. After that for a time there was no rule on the subject, but in the second session of the Fifty-second Congress[1] a rule was adopted which makes it the duty of the several committees to report the general appropriation bills within eighty days after the formation of the committees in a long session, and within forty days after the commencement of a short session; and further provides that "in failure thereof, the reasons of such failure shall be privileged for consideration, when called for by any member of the House."

Of late years the senate usually increases the amount of the appropriations: the bills of the house providing for an amount less than that demanded by the estimates of the heads of the departments, are raised in the senate so as to correspond more nearly to them. The result is that the senate has come to be accused of extravagance. According to Mr. Sherman, another reason why appropriations are always increased in the senate is that the heads of the various departments, for some reason, perhaps a

[1] Rules of the House, No. XI, sec. 53.

desire to appear economical, never include in their estimates all of their expenses, and when the appropriation bills are before the senate committee they appear and ask to have these items inserted.

The right of amendment of the appropriation bills granted to the senate by the constitution, has always been given the broadest interpretation; the only limitation upon it being the rules of the senate. At first there was no need of rules. During the first twenty years only about one-half of the appropriation bills received any amendment at all.[1] The house generally agreed to these amendments of the senate, and when it did not, the senate receded.[2] Conference committees were, therefore, not often necessary, there being but six on appropriation bills during the first thirty years.

Later it became the custom to discuss on the appropriation bills more than any others, the questions that concerned the country at large, and numerous amendments, containing general legislation or providing for private claims,[3] were added, so that half of the debates on appropriation bills came to be concerned with these private claims.[4] This state of affairs caused the

[1] Out of thirty-three general appropriation bills seven passed the senate without amendment. Of twenty-two army appropriation bills thirteen, and of the fifteen navy appropriation bills twelve passed the senate without amendment. During the next ten years an increasing number of the appropriation bills were amended, about two-thirds being so treated.

[2] Of the twenty-four general appropriation bills amended by the senate, the house concurred in all the amendments made to eighteen of them, and in certain of the amendments made to the other six; and it concurred in all of the amendments of the senate to the nine army and three navy bills which the senate amended. As neither the amendments made by the senate, nor the bills as first passed by the house, are generally given, it is impossible to tell how important the senate amendments were.

[3] Congr. Globe, 1st Sess., 32d Congr., p. 1287, statement of Mr. Bright.

[4] *Ibid.*, p. 2170, statement of Mr. Hunter.

adoption, without debate, in 1850 of a rule which provided that: "No amendment proposing an additional appropriation shall be received to any general appropriation bill, unless it be made to carry out the provisions of some existing law, or some act or resolution previously passed by the Senate during the session, or in pursuance of an estimate from the head of some of the departments; and no amendment shall be received whose object is to provide for a private claim, although the same may have been previously sanctioned by the Senate."[1] A little later this rule was amended so as to allow amendments proposed by a standing committee, it being urged that otherwise the senate could but register the decrees of the house. The same privilege was later extended to select committees.[2] The rule was again amended in 1854 by striking out "although the same may have been previously sanctioned by the Senate," and inserting "unless it be to carry out the provisions of an existing law or treaty stipulation,"[3] and again, in 1867, the rule was further modified by adding: "and all amendments to general appropriation bills reported from the Committees of the Senate, proposing new items of appropriation, shall, one day before they are offered, be referred to the Committee

[1] Congr. Globe, vol. 23, 2d Sess., 31st Congr., p. 94. The rule as interpreted by the senate was construed to apply to estimates made by he departments at the request of individual senators, and to an amendment proposed by a committee, and based on an estimate of a department. (Congr. Globe, 1st Sess., 32d Congr., pp. 1190, 1192.) A motion made in 1852 to require the recommendation of an appropriation by the head of the department to which it referred was not adopted. (*Ibid.*, pp. 1286–87.)

[2] Congr. Globe, 1st Sess., 33d Congr., p. 1381.

[3] *Ibid.*, p. 1058. The same session (p. 2214), a proposal was made, but not voted on, which declared that "hereafter the Senate will not receive or consider any bill or proposition, other than the general appropriation bills for the support of the government, which appropriates money for more than one object."

on Appropriations; and all general appropriation bills shall be referred to the same Committee."[1]

Under the old rule it had been held that an amendment to an amendment could be offered by anybody,[2] and the presiding officer thought this the correct interpretation under the new rule, but his decision was overruled.[3]

Prior to 1855, there had been no instance of important general legislation being attached to appropriation bills, though for the preceding ten years unimportant legislation had been passed in that way. In that year the tariff bill was added to an appropriation bill,[4] and from that time on such a course of procedure became very common.[5] Mr. Sherman, speaking of the practice in the Fortieth Congress, said: "Almost every legislative act changes an existing law, and the House rule forbids that being done on the appropriation bills; but in the Senate we have never practiced upon that. On the contrary, we seek the appropriation bills, sometimes, not only to carry convenient amendments, but to assert great principles; and I might go to many instances in the history of the government where the Senate has attached important legislative provisions to appropriation bills, and has presented them in that way forcibly to the country."[6]

Proposals made at the second sessions of the Fortieth and Forty-first Congresses, for such amendments of the rules as to forbid general legislation on the appropriation bills, were rejected or tabled;[7] but in the second session

[1] Congr. Globe, 1st Sess., 40th Congr., p. 12.

[2] *Ibid.*, p. 3518, decision of the Chair.

[3] *Ibid.*, p. 3520.

[4] *Ibid.*, 2d Sess., 33d Congr.

[5] Prominent examples are to be found in the second session of the 34th Congress, the second session of the 38th Congress, and the first sessions of the 39th and 42d Congresses.

[6] Congr. Globe, 2d Sess., 40th Congr., p. 3612.

[7] *Ibid.*, 2d Sess., 40th Congr., pp. 2089, 2090, and 2d Sess., 41st Congr., pp. 4128, 4249.

of the Forty-second Congress, the tendency to put all the legislation of the session on the appropriation bills led the senate to adopt a resolution not to receive, during the remainder of the session, any amendments making legislative provisions other than such as directly related to the appropriations contained in the bill.[1] No permanent change, however, was made until the second session of the Forty-fourth Congress,[2] when it was provided that no amendment to a general appropriation bill should be received which proposed general legislation, or which was not germane or relevant to the subject-matter of the bill.[3] This rule was held to apply to general legislation sent from the house, and to amendments of conference committees.[4]

Prior to this time the rules of the house on the subject had been more strict than those of the senate, and the house was accustomed, therefore, when it wished something forbidden by its rules to be included in an appropriation bill, to get it put on in the senate. Now this was changed.[5] There was, however, no less of general legislation on appropriation bills, for the point of order would either be waived and legislation allowed, or all general legislation would be stricken out, and then, in conference committee, part of it would be put back on without the senate ever having discussed it. Thus Mr. Blaine said, in 1879, that there had been more legislation on appropriation bills since the adoption of the senate rule than in the twenty previous years, because, the

[1] Congr. Globe, 2d Sess.. 42d Congr., p. 2883, yeas 33, nays 13.

[2] Proposals had, however, been earlier made for such a change, as in the first session of the 44th Congr., pp. 1362, 2100.

[3] Congr. Record, 2d Sess., 44th Congress, p. 628, rule 29.

[4] *Ibid.*, 1st Sess., 47th Congr., p. 6603; 2d Sess., 48th Congr., p. 1467. For other decisions under the rule, see 2d Sess., 46th Congr., Sen. Misc. Docs., vol. II, No. 84, under rule 29.

[5] Statement of Mr. Dawes, Congr. Record, 2d Sess., 48th Congr., p. 1465.

senate being restricted by its rules, the house had it all its own way;[1] and in the Forty-eighth Congress, Mr. Ingalls declared that, for the last ten years, there had hardly been an appropriation bill passed which did not contain general legislation.[2]

A joint rule on the subject, adopted by the senate in the first session of the Forty-eighth Congress, was not agreed to by the house,[3] but the house in the first session of the Forty-ninth Congress amended its rules so as not to allow the change of any existing law on an appropriation bill.[4] This rule, which was interpeted by Speaker Reed so as to forbid all legislation on the appropriation bills, has turned the tables, and greatly increased the power of the senate, so that now, as at an earlier period, if the house wishes general legislation on an appropriation bill it must get it put on in the senate, where a majority only is required to suspend the rules after notice given, while in the house two-thirds is necessary.

## VI. PARTY INFLUENCES IN THE SENATE.

In spite of the secondary election of senators, which it might be supposed would remove them to a certain extent from party politics, party influences began to make themselves felt in the senate as soon as parties were organized. As the state legislatures almost invariably elected men belonging to the party dominant in those bodies, a senator was as much the representative of a party as if

[1] Congr. Record, 3d Sess., 45th Congr., p. 635.

[2] Congr. Record, 2d Sess., 48th Congr., p. 1318.

[3] A proposal in the first session of the Fiftieth Congress for a rule directing the presiding officer on the receipt of house bills to strike out all provisions of a "general legislative character other than such as relate to the dispositions of the moneys appropriated therein," subject, however, to an appeal to the senate, was not agreed to. (Congr. Record, p. 4208.)

[4] P. 332. Previously it had been allowed if it restricted expenditure and was germane to the subject.

he had been elected directly. Of the extent to which party feeling was carried one may judge from a letter of Jefferson in 1797 to Rutledge, in which he says: "You and I have formerly seen warm debates and high political passions. But gentlemen of different politics would then speak to each other, and separate the business of the Senate from that of Society. It is not so now. Men who have been intimate all their lives, cross the street to avoid meeting, and turn their heads the other way, lest they should be obliged to touch their hats."[1]

It is difficult to tell just when party caucuses to decide upon the vote of the party on legislative measures came into use. During Washington's administration, they were held to decide on the action of the party regarding nominations;[2] and it is a well established fact that a secret caucus was held in 1800, for nominating a presidential candidate. The same year it was declared by Duane, in his paper, that a legislative party caucus was held at the house of one of the senators, at which seventeen senators were present; and he further states that caucuses were then in use in the senate, and that a certain bill, called the electoral count bill, was framed in a caucus to which Mr. Pinckney, a staunch Republican, and one of the committee to whom the bill was referred, was not bidden.[3] Mr. Pinckney, however, declared that he was present at all the meetings of the committee, and the report of the committee to whom the accusation was referred declared it "false, defamatory, scandalous, and malicious, tending to defame the Senators of the United States, to bring them into contempt and disrepute, and

[1] Works, vol. IV, p. 191.

[2] Davis, Life of Burr, I, p. 408. This was to decide whom to suggest to Washington as ambassador to France. Again in 1799, a caucus of Federal senators was held to decide whether to reject the nomination of Vans Murray to France. (Hamilton's Works, ed. by J. C. Hamilton, VI, 400.)

[3] Annals of Congress, 1st Sess., 6th Congr., p. 114.

to excite against them the hatred of the good people of the United States."

If the statement of Duane was false, it would still seem that legislative party caucuses came in but a short time afterwards, for Bradford, speaking of the second session of the Eighth Congress, says: "During this session there was far less of free and independent discussion on the measures proposed by the friends of the administration, than had been previously practised in both branches of the national legislature. It appeared that on the most important subjects the course adopted by the majority was the effect of caucus arrangement or, in other words, had been previously agreed upon at meetings of the Democratic members held in private. Thus, the legislation of congress was constantly swayed by party feelings and pledges, rather than according to sound reason, or personal conviction."[1] This system of party dictation was continued. In 1809, Story, giving his reasons for refusing a re-election to the senate, writes: "I found an entire obedience to party projects required such constant sacrifices of opinion and feeling, that my solicitude was greatly increased to withdraw from the field."[2]

The use of the caucus constantly increased. After a time, as has been seen, the committees were always decided upon in caucus. Sometimes the order of business was decided there.[3] In 1862 an attempt was even made to control the president in his choice of cabinet officers, by a decree of the caucus advising the displacement of Seward, the secretary of state. Seward immediately resigned, but as the rest of the cabinet declared that they

[1] Williams, Statesman's Manual, I, 244, quoting Bradford, History of Federal Government.

[2] Life of Story, I, 194, 195.

[3] In the 1st session of the 40th Congr., (pp. 496 ff.) there was a discussion of caucus obligations, owing to Mr. Sumner's holding, contrary to the generally accepted theory, that one who remained in the caucus was not necessarily bound by its decisions.

would resign rather than consent to the proposed change, and as when the news got abroad it was received with general disapproval, the caucus began to back down, and the President requested Seward to resume the office which he had resigned.

The caucus of the senate now usually meets about twice a month, and it is very largely through it that the older members in the senate exercise such a preponderating influence.

Another restriction upon the freedom of the early senators was the instructions of their state legislatures. The states had been accustomed to instruct their representatives to the continental congress, and there had been some discussion in the convention as to whether the senators should be independent of their legislatures, or should receive instructions from them. The right of instruction was debated in the house during the first session of the First Congress; but it was not until the third session that the question was brought up in the senate by a motion of the Virginia senators, in obedience to their instructions, which they mentioned, for opening the doors of the senate. Various opinions regarding instructions were expressed. It was held that they amounted to no more than a wish, and ought to be no further regarded; that they were binding upon senators; that no legislature had any right to instruct at all, any more than the electors had a right to instruct the president; that in local questions affecting the interests of his constituents the representative ought to obey his instructions, but that in a national question he should not consider himself bound by the wishes of his constituents.

There was a second discussion of the question in 1808, but the most considerable debate on the subject in the senate, and the one in which the views of the opposite parties were most fully set forth, arose in connection with the re-charter of the United States bank (1811), upon which certain of the large states had instructed their representatives how to vote. Some senators obeyed their instructions and some did not; but all felt it necessary to explain their action, and the reasons for it. Thus the debates were long drawn out, and the same thing said over and over again, but without any decision being reached.

The subjects for which instructions were used were various. They were used, as in the case of the bank bill, to enforce the wishes of the states on important questions; or to propose amendments to the constitution; or to secure the passage of a local bill. The usual form of these instructions was: "*Resolved*, That the Senators of this state, in the Congress of the United States, be instructed, and our Representatives most earnestly requested," etc. Sometimes they were sent in the form of wishes only, or as requests. The results of instructions were usually satisfactory. Often the senators agreed with them, or could, on receiving them, make themselves believe that they did; and, if they did not, enough pressure was usually brought to bear to make them prefer to resign rather than stay in office in direct opposition to the will of their constituents.

The case of Hugh L. White attracted a good deal of attention. Benton, in speaking of his resignation, writes that it took place "under circumstances not frequent, but sometimes occurring in the Senate, . . . that of receiving instructions from the general assembly of his state, which either operate as a censure upon a senator or which require him to do something which either his conscience or his honor forbids." He continues: "He consulted his self-respect, as well as obeyed a Democratic principle, and sent in his resignation."

A later instance of similar action is the resignation of Brown and Strange, senators from North Carolina, in

1840. An opposite interpretation of the relations of senators to the state legislatures was given by Sumner in 1872, when censured by the Massachusetts legislature.

State legislatures are still accustomed to communicate to their representatives their views on various matters, and to instruct or request[1] senators to act in a certain way.

Sometimes, still, a senator is seen voting for a measure of which he disapproves, giving as a reason for his action that the measure is favored by the state which he represents.

It was natural that those states which held that state legislatures had a right to issue to senators mandatory instructions, should also wish to have the power to recall them; and Virginia, in 1808, did in fact instruct her representatives to procure such an amendment to the constitution.[2] Attempts were also made to make senators more dependent upon their constituents by shortening their term of office.

## VII. RELATION OF THE PRESIDENT AND SENATE IN LEGISLATION.

Although it is in the performance of its executive duties that the senate comes most in contact with the president, yet in the execution of its legislative duties the influence of the president is also felt.

The only authorized means for the exercise of this influence is through the veto, and the right and duty of the president from time to time to give "to the Congress Information of the state of the Union, and recommend to their Consideration such Measures as he shall judge necessary and expedient."[3] This the president has done in his annual and special messages, both of which are now

[1] For examples of this form see 1st Sess., 43d Congr., Sen. Misc. Docs., Nos. 61, 69.

[2] Sen. Jour., 1st Sess., 10th Congr., p. 267. Tenn. and N. J. passed resolutions against this.

[3] Art. II, sec. III.

written. The annual messages of Washington and Adams, however, were delivered in the senate chamber where the house was also assembled, and a formal answer was returned by both houses, who waited upon the president for this purpose.

Before the introduction of standing committees the various portions of the president's annual message were referred to special committees; afterwards they were referred to the standing committees having the subject in charge as were also the special messages and reports.

As the president can not support his plans in the senate and has no means of enforcing them, they amount to little more than suggestions which congress may follow or not as it sees fit.

The considerable influence on legislation which some presidents have exercised seems usually to have been mainly due to some circumstance other than their occupation of the presidential chair, such as their popularity with the people or their position as the recognized leaders of their party.

The influence of the first few presidents on legislation was very considerable; but, with the decline in the character of the occupants of the office, their influence on legislation has decreased, and this in spite of the use of the patronage to support it and the increased use of the veto power. The first considerable use of the veto was made by Jackson, who vetoed eleven bills, a greater number than had been vetoed in the forty preceding years.[1] As a result it became no unusual thing to use the prediction of a veto as a chief argument in debate. Clay, in a speech on the removal of the deposits, said: "The question is no longer what laws will Congress pass, but what will the Executive not veto? The President, and not Congress, is addressed for legislative action."[2]

[1] Prior to Jackson there had been but nine vetoes.

[2] Congr. Debates, vol. X, part 1, 1st Sess., 23d Congr., p. 94.

Tyler and Johnson by their use of the veto set themselves in opposition to the will of congress; and, as under Tyler it was impossible to pass bills over his veto, great deference was paid to his wishes in the hopes of securing his assent; but, as under Johnson the majority was large enough to override his vetoes, he was able by this means to exercise but little influence.

The use of the veto to defeat other than unconstitutional legislation was first objected to during the administration of Jackson.[1] It had, without question, been extended by former presidents to inexpedient legislation;[2] and the popular appeals on the subject, beginning in 1832 and running down to 1844, resulted in a verdict in favor of a large and liberal discretion on the part of the executive in the exercise of this power.

Prior to Cleveland's time the veto power had, in the main, been exercised only upon theoretical propositions or political questions; and his liberal application of it to special and individual legislation, especially to pension cases and public buildings, aroused considerable opposition. Some held that the president had no right to exercise this power on a mere question of fact, such as whether a given pension ought to be granted, and that it was not the duty of the president to veto every bill which he should vote against were he a member of congress. Cleveland's action, however, has been approved and applauded by the country.

As under Jackson the control of the legislature by the use of the veto was greatly increased, so, during his presidency, is seen the beginning of the use of patronage for the same purpose,—a means of influence which has constantly increased, though checked by the Civil Service Reform, which diminished the number of offices to be disposed of by the president.

[1] Clay's Works, V, 524. Webster, Works, IV, 86. Congr. Globe, 1st Sess., 30th Congr., p. 898.

[2] Madison, IV, 369. Story, Commentaries, sec. 887.

The chief influence of the president on legislation is exercised through the heads of the departments who, unlike those of the continental congress, are responsible to the president only and not to congress. At first, with one exception, the cabinet officers were assigned no duties toward congress. The secretary of the treasury, however, was required to "digest and prepare plans, to report estimates and give information in person or in writing to either branch of Congress on subjects relating to his department."[1] Objections had been made to allowing the secretary to report in person, because it was feared that he would then be able to exert too much influence; and this reason was doubtless influential in causing the senate, when Hamilton was about to make his report on the national finances, and asked whether it should be made in person or in writing, to decide in favor of the latter.

Other members of the cabinet, during the Frst Congress, appeared in the senate chamber. The secretary of foreign affairs was twice summoned to appear before the senate.[2] The president on several occasions sent messages by his secretaries;[3] and, in one instance, General Knox, on two successive days, accompanied the president

[1] Statutes at Large, 1st Sess., 1st Congr., chap. 12, sec. 2. The reason for the different constitution of this department does not appear in the debates, but Gallatin suggests that its object was to give to congress direct control over financial matters (Works, I, 67); which may also account for the fact that while the titles of the other acts establishing the departments read "An Act to establish an Executive Department to be denominated," etc., that of the treasury reads simply "An Act to establish a Treasury Department."

[2] Exec. Jour., vol. I, pp. 6, 7.

[3] In the 1st Sess., 1st Congr., two messages were sent by Jay (Sen. Jour., I, 89, 93), and six by General Knox (Exec. Jour., I, 3, 26, 34; Sen. Jour., I, 55, 56, 81). At the next session four messages were sent by General Knox (Exec. Jour., I, 36, 58; Sen. Jour., I, 105, 107).

in the senate chamber; but with these exceptions no ministers have attended in the senate.[1] A unanimous report of a committee of eight senators in February, 1881, in favor of giving to members of the cabinet seats in both houses and recommending a change in the rules to provide for this, has never been acted upon.

The secretary of foreign affairs, whose office was first created, has always been considered as at the head of the cabinet; though for some time after the organization of the government, owing to the deplorable condition of the finances and the importance of their regulation, and perhaps also to the character of the occupants of the office, the duties of the secretary of the treasury were more important. While the office was held by Hamilton and Gallatin, it exercised the most influence on legislation, and it was through it mainly that the executive influence was exerted.

Before Hamilton entered upon his duties congress had been awkwardly struggling with the revenue, and when he was appointed, it turned eagerly to him for assistance. Not only were the plans submitted by him usually adopted but others were demanded of him. Frequent calls for information were also made, and a couple of the replies of Hamilton to such requests, which he considered demanded too much, show a boldness and independ-

[1] So far as I have been able to discover, these were the only instances in which secretaries attended in the senate, but Benton says, in his "Abridgement of the Debates of Congress" (I, 16, note): "These entries in relation to the Secretary of Foreign Affairs show the early method of communicating with the Secretaries, being called before the Senate to give explanations and bring papers—a method now superseded by reports. The early Senators lamented the change, believing the old way to be the best for getting the information that was wanted, and also the best security against the appointment of incompetent Secretaries." And Woodrow Wilson says in his "Congressional Government" (p. 257): "Before the Republican reaction which followed the supremacy of the Federalists the heads of the departments appeared in person before the houses to impart desired information and to make what suggestions they might have to venture."

ence which a cabinet officer of the present time would hardly dare assume.[1] Jefferson, who, it must be remembered, was an opponent of Hamilton, early thought that his department had an undue influence over the members of the legislature.[2]

During the civil war the importance of the secretary of the treasury again became great, and his influence ever since has been considerable.

The treasury department being so important in the First Congress, the need of annual reports from it was felt earlier than in the other departments. Hamilton had been accustomed to send in a statement of the expenses for the past fiscal year, together with an estimate of the accountant. As this was found inadequate it was later provided: "That it shall be the duty of the Secretary of the Treasury to digest, to prepare, and to lay before Congress at the commencement of every session, a report on the subject of finance, containing estimates of the public revenue and public expenditures, and plans for improving or increasing the revenues from time to time, for the purpose of giving information to Congress in adopting modes of raising money requisite to meet the public expenditures."[3] As time went on statutes were passed making annual reports to congress on other subjects obligatory. A little later annual reports from the other departments were also demanded.

Besides the annual reports of the secretaries the senate is accustomed to ask for special reports on subjects relating to their departments. These calls for information are most frequent. Even during the earlier years they were numerous enough to occasion considerable inconvenience, and in later times they have led to propo-

[1] Works, ed. by J. C. Hamilton, III, pp. 447, 588. Report of Feb. 6, 1794.

[2] Jefferson, Works, III, 461, and IX, 95.

[3] Statutes at Large, II, 80.

sals for the restriction of this unlimited right.[1] Sometimes the secretaries are not only asked for facts, but also for opinions,[2] and sometimes even for the project of a bill.

Besides the calls made by the senate itself, frequent calls are also made by the committees; and, especially of late, it is mainly through these that the senate obtains what information it wants, and that the influence of the secretaries is exerted. Either the chairman or some member of the committee will call upon the secretary to obtain the desired information, or the secretary will be summoned before the committee to give his opinions or to make explanations and defend his plans. Sometimes also the secretaries are called upon for projects of bills. In later years they are not accustomed to wait for the committee to call upon them for their opinions, but themselves take the initiative, either waiting upon the committee or its chairman or some member of the committee for this purpose. Sometimes a secretary acts directly upon the senate by inducing some senator to introduce a bill framed in his department.[3]

The influence which the executive department is able

[1] As for a rule requiring all calls to be referred to a committee before they were voted upon (Congr. Globe, 2d Sess., 40th Congress, p. 2090), and for a rule requiring resolutions to lie over one day, which Mr. Webster said was caused by the increased practice of making calls upon the departments.

[2] Hamilton especially was frequently asked for his opinions. Objections were made to such calls on the ground that they gave an undue influence to the secretary; and, at the second session of the Twenty-second Congress (Congr. Deb., vol. IX, part i, 11, 27, 50–59), the senate refused to make such a call, though at the previous session such a call had been made. In the second session of the Twenty-fifth Congress, the senate again refused to call for opinions. (Congr. Globe, pp. 58, 59.)

[3] For example, the Mills Tariff Bill, the Fishery Bill, and the Chinese Exclusion Bill.

to exert upon legislation by all these means is very considerable.[1]

### VIII. RELATIONS OF THE SENATE AND HOUSE OF REPRESENTATIVES IN LEGISLATION.

The first senate manifested many aristocratic tendencies. The majority wished to establish a government which should be dignified and awe inspiring. This appeared very prominently in the debates over the titles to be applied to the president and vice president,[2] which occupied the senate for nearly a month, and the discussion over the manner in which senators should be referred to in the minutes.[3] The senate did not forget that it was the upper branch of the legislature and, in various ways, showed that it felt itself superior to the house. Thus when a bill was received from the house which began: "Be it enacted by the Congress of the United States," it was amended in the senate to read: "Be it enacted by the Senate and House of Representatives," Senator Izard declaring that the "dignity and preëminence of the Senate was the thing aimed at" in the form adopted by the house.[4]

The same disposition was again shown when the mode of communication between the two houses was under consideration. A committee of the two houses, after consultation, agreed to a report which provided for the sending of all bills to the house by the secretary of the senate, but required the house to send bills to the senate by two of its members and all other messages by one member.[5] The house refusing to agree to this, and an-

[1] See 3d Sess., 46th Congr., Sen. Reports, No. 837. Report of a committee of eight senators in favor of allowing secretaries a seat in the senate and house of representatives.

[2] Annals of Congress, 1st Sess., 1st Congr., pp. 34, 35, 36.

[3] Journal of Maclay, pp. 64, 65.

[4] *Ibid.*, p. 16.

[5] Annals of Congress, 1st Sess., 1st Congr., pp. 23, 24.

other conference failing to bring about a compromise, the senate agreed to receive messages by the clerk of the house, until a rule regulating the mode of procedure was adopted; and it was finally left to each house to send messages by the persons whom a sense of propriety would dictate.

The senate was again forced to give up its pretensions when the subject of the salaries which the members of congress should receive was under consideration. The house bill provided for the same compensation for senators and representatives, but in the senate it was voted, thirteen to six, that there ought to be a discrimination.[1] A substitute for the house bill was then adopted which, while leaving the salary of senators and representatives the same until 1795, provided that, thereafter, the salary of the former should be a dollar a day more. The house refused to agree to this, and a bill regulating the salary until 1795, and granting the same compensation to members of the two houses, was finally adopted.[2] When the question was again brought up in 1895 the senate no longer made any claims for a higher salary.

The practice of the British parliament, where the two houses were entirely independent of each other, was followed, as a matter of course, in the congress of the United States;[3] it always being considered out of order to refer in one house to the debates, votes, or majorities in the other.[4] A resolution, introduced in the senate by Mr. Hoar, in the first session of the Forty-ninth Congress, declaring that it was not out of order, when a private bill was under consideration, to read or refer to a report on the same subject made in the house of representatives

[1] Sen. Jour., I, 66.
[2] *Ibid.*, I, 66, 67.
[3] Jefferson's Manual, sec. XVII.
[4] *Ibid.*

during the same congress,[1] was referred to the committee on rules and not brought before the senate again.

Since the careful reporting and publication of the proceedings of congress, so that what is done in one body is immediately known everywhere, this prohibition against reference to debates practically amounts to nothing;[2] and the influence of the action of each house on the other, which has always existed,[3] has greatly increased; this being due largely to the increased knowledge in each house of the proceedings of the other.[4]

On certain subjects of minor detail which involve no question of public policy, the two houses act by joint committees.[5] Occasionally also a joint committee on more important matters has been appointed. Such was the joint committee appointed to consider the expediency of admitting Missouri into the Union, and that to consider the expediency of a change of Indian policy.[6] Still more important were the joint committees on reconstruction created after the civil war.

In the early days it was also customary, toward the close of a session, to appoint a joint committee to decide

[1] Congr. Record, 1st Sess., 49th Congr., 5493. Mr. Hoar said that the proposed rule embodied the recent practice of the senate.

[2] *Ibid.*, pp. 54, 93.

[3] In 1790 Mr. Page said that, occasionally, there were heard in the house such expressions as "We hear that the senate did so and so," and that the argument that the senate would not agree to certain things was often used in the house. (*Penn. Packet*, July 15, 1790.) In 1840, the fact that an appropriation bill had been thoroughly discussed in the house was given, in the senate, as a reason for its immediate passage (Congr. Globe, 1st Sess., 26th Congr., p. 375); and in the first session of the Forty-first Congress Mr. Pomeroy said: "It is a constantly growing practice here in the Senate—it was not so formerly but it has become so within the last year or two—to threaten us with the action of the House; to tell us that if you do so and so the House will not agree to it, and if you do so and so the President or some other department will not agree to it." (Congr. Globe, p. 25.)

[4] So says Mr. Hale, Congr. Record, 1st Sess., 49th Congr., pp. 54, 93.

[5] As committee on engrossed bills, committee on the library.

[6] Congr. Globe, 2d Sess., 41st Congr., p. 2639.

on the time for adjournment and the business which should be acted upon during the remainder of the session. This came to be objected to, both because of its inexpediency and uselessness, as the committee usually recommended new subjects to be considered instead of those which had already been matured in one house,[1] and the recommendations were usually disregarded; and because the business of the two houses ought not to be mixed.[2]

The most important of all the joint committees are the committees of conference, for to them now are usually referred all the important matters which come before congress. The power of the conference committees is very great, especially near the end of the session when there is no time to examine their report, and it is unusual for the report even to be read, it being adopted or rejected on the recommendation of the chairman, who gives a brief statement of its contents. Even that, however, is sometimes omitted.

Although the senate was, with one exception, given the same legislative power as the house, the most important measures were generally introduced in the house, in the early days; and the house was much more active than the senate in the initiation of legislation. Thus in the First Congress the house passed and sent to the senate about six times as many bills as the senate to the house, and of the bills which became laws about the same proportion were introduced in the house. The work of revision and amendment of the house bills, to which the senate devoted more time than to the originating of bills of its own, was carefully and thoroughly done, as shown by the number of amendments made to the house bills and by the accounts of the debates given

[1] Congr. Deb., vol. IV, part 1, 1st Sess., 20th Congr., p. 690.
[2] *Ibid.*, p. 691.

in "Maclay's Journal."[1] The senate, however, did not long leave to the house such a preponderating part in the origination of legislation. Its activity gradually increased, and, in the Tenth Congress, while the senate introduced and passed fifty-four bills, the house introduced and passed but eighty-one. From that time until recently the proportion has remained about the same in general, though sometimes, as in the Twentieth Congress,[2] the number of its own bills passed by the senate has nearly equaled the number of house bills passed by the house, and occasionally, as in the special session of the Fortieth Congress the senate has even surpassed the house in the number of its own bills which it has passed.[3] At the Forty-ninth, Fiftieth, and Fifty-first Congresses the number of senate bills passed by the senate nearly equalled the number of house bills passed by the house, and in the Fifty-second Congress surpassed it.[4]

The proportion of house and senate bills that have become laws has been about the same as the proportion of its own bills passed by each house, except that the recent increase in the number of its own bills passed by the senate has not been accompanied by a corresponding increase in the number of senate bills which have become laws. Up to this time, though the house had not passed as many senate bills as the senate had house bills, the house had passed about as large a proportion of the senate bills sent it, as the senate of the house bills; but now, while the senate sends to the house nearly as many or even more bills than the house to the senate, about three times as many house bills have become laws.

[1] During the first session of the First Congress the senate amended all but two of the house bills in which it concurred.

[2] At the first session of the Twentieth Congress the senate passed 119 of its own bills and the house 132 of its.

[3] The senate passed 31 of its bills and the house 24 of its.

[4] Congr. Record, 1st Sess., 52d Congr., vol. 23, part I, pp. 820, 821; *Public Opinion*, April 12, 1894.

Usually bills were taken up in their order, preference being given to neither senate nor house bills;[1] but the great increase in the amount of business, and the failure of the house to act upon anything like all the bills sent it by the senate, has of late led, on several occasions, to the adoption of a resolution giving preference to house bills.[2] This was advocated on the ground that there were already on the house table more senate bills than it could possibly act upon, and objected to because it would increase the discrimination already existing between the two houses, in regard to the origination of bills, until the house would claim, as practically its prerogative, the introduction of all bills. A joint rule, proposed by the senate, providing that each house during the last days of the session, in proceeding with the calendar, should take up the business from the other,[3] was not adopted by the house; and thus each house is still left free to do as it likes.

From the time of the great debate over the Missouri Compromise, until the end of the civil war, most of the important measures were introduced in the senate;[4] but, since the war, and the settlement of the great problems of reconstruction, the questions of most importance to the nation being those of an economic nature, the senate has now lost its preëminence in this respect.

[1] A motion made in the first session of the Sixteenth Congress for a rule which practically would have given the preference to house bills was laid on the table. (Congr. Deb., vol. I, p. 613.) At the second session of the Seventeenth Congress preference was given to senate bills. (Annals of Congr., p. 288.)

[2] Congr. Record, 3d Sess., 46th Congr., pp. 2108, 2109; 2d Sess., 48th Congr., pp. 303, 304, 1707.

[3] *Ibid.*, 1st Sess., 49th Congr., p. 186, Rule 10.

[4] For example, the measures regarding Texas and Oregon, the admission of Iowa and Florida, the Kansas and Nebraska Bills.

# CHAPTER IV.

## THE SENATE AS AN EXECUTIVE BODY.

### I. SECRET SESSIONS.

IN the early days, when all the sessions of the senate were held behind closed doors, the distinction, now very important, of the admission or non-admission of the public to the respective sessions, was absent. While the legislative sessions were soon made public, the executive sessions have constantly tended toward greater secrecy.

Though at first all business was transacted with closed doors, there was no rule requiring it to be kept secret; and that it was not so considered is evident, in spite of the fact that Maclay says the contrary,[1] from the fact that it was thought necessary to impose a special injunction of secrecy whenever it was desired to keep anything from the public. Moreover, the legislative business could not have been regarded as secret, since provision was at once made for its monthly publication.[2] This order related to the legislative proceedings only, and at the same time it was ordered that the proceedings in executive session should be recorded in a separate book. There are, however, some indications that the executive proceedings were also published. Thus at the first session of the First Congress provision was made for sending "a printed copy of the Journals of both Houses, at the end of every session of Congress, to the Executive of each State and to the Legislature thereof;"[3] and in 1792 a resolution was adopted by the senate

[1] Rule XI given by Mr. Maclay provides: "Inviolable secrecy shall be observed with respect to all matters transacted in the Senate, while the doors are shut, or as often as the same is enjoined from the Chair."

[2] Sen. Jour., vol. I, p. 27.

[3] Annals of Congress, 1st Sess., 1st Congr., p. 96.

in executive session providing "That no executive business in the future be published by the Secretary of the Senate."[1] A resolution proposed in 1791, authorizing the secretary of the senate to "furnish the members of the Senate, when required, with extracts of such parts of the Executive Journal as are not, by vote of the Senate, considered secret,"[2] would indicate that the "Executive Journal" was not considered secret; and later, we find senators maintaining that it was open to inspection.[3] In 1806, however, in the revision of the rules it was provided that extracts from the executive records should not be furnished except by special order.[4]

Motions for opening the doors of the senate to the public, which, beginning with the second session of the First Congress, were renewed in every subsequent session until the desired object was attained, provided for so doing only when the senate was acting in its legislative, or legislative and judicial capacities. Apparently no one desired open sessions when executive business was being transacted.

The first rule imposing secrecy was not passed until the twenty-second of December, 1800, some time after the legislative business had been transacted in public. This rule, suggested by President Adams at a time when foreign relations were threatening, provided: "That all confidential communications made by the President of the United States to the Senate, shall be, by the members thereof, kept inviolably secret; and that all treaties which may hereafter be laid before the Senate, shall also be kept secret, until the Senate shall, by their resolution, take off the injunction of secrecy."[5]

1 Exec. Jour., I, 100.

2 Res. of January 21, 1791, which was never called up. (Annals of Congr., p. 1792).

3 Annals of Congress, 2d Sess., 7th Congr., pp. 38, 39.

4 Annals of Congress, 1st Sess., 9th Congr., p. 203, Rule 32.

5 Exec. Jour., vol. I, p. 361.

At first all papers communicated by the president upon executive business were held to be confidential,[1] but after 1830 only such communications as were marked "confidential" were so considered.[2] The senate had earlier decided, in connection with the Panama mission, that it had a right to publish confidential communications of the president, and to discuss them in public, without the assent of the president, whenever they thought the public interest required it.[3] John Quincy Adams, who at that time was president, declared such a course to be unprecedented.[4]

For some time there was no rule regarding secrecy in the consideration of nominations and they were communicated by senators without reserve.[5] Proposals, made in 1813, for the adoption of a rule imposing secrecy upon nominations were not considered;[6] and it was not until 1820 that it was ordered that "All information or remarks, touching or concerning the character or qualifications of any person nominated by the President to office," should be considered secret.[7] It would seem, however, that, before this, it had come to be the custom to keep such matters secret; for, a couple of years earlier when the proceedings which took place in the senate on a certain nomination were desired as evidence in the courts, the resolution which it was thought necessary to introduce authorizing senators to relate those proceedings, was voted for by one senator only.[8] The rule adopted in 1820 was interpreted as imposing secrecy upon the votes of individuals, since they were the expression of

[1] Congr. Deb., vol. II, p. 145, and Exec. Jour., vol. IV, p. 122.
[2] Exec. Jour., vol. IV, pp. 122 ff.
[3] Congr. Deb., vol. II, p. 147.
[4] *Ibid.*, p. 146, and J. Q. Adams, Works, vol. VII, p. 117.
[5] Annals of Congress, 2d Sess., 7th Congr., p. 49.
[6] Exec. Jour., II, 374, 392.
[7] Rule 37.
[8] Exec. Jour., III, 114.

an opinion, but not upon the fact of nomination, confirmation, or rejection, or the state of the vote, nor was it held to contain a prohibition against each senator telling how he had himself voted.[1]

The removal of the injunction of secrecy is now more common than in the early days. Prior to 1828 it was of rare occurrence, and confined principally to the proceedings on treaties or nominations, and seldom extended to documents.[2]

For a long time there was no provision for giving a nominee an opportunity to defend himself against any charges brought forward; but in 1877 it was provided that, when such charges were made, the committee might, at its discretion, notify such nominee thereof, but the name of the person making such charges should not be disclosed.[3] Under this rule it became the custom, when serious charges were made against a nominee, to allow him an opportunity to defend himself.

Despite the injunctions and rules imposing secrecy, what is transacted in executive session has always become known. Thus, Mr. Forsyth said in 1831 that: "It was soon found, as the Government moved on, that if a desire was felt that any subject should be bruited about in every corner of the United States, should become a topic of universal conversation, nothing more was necessary than to close the doors of the Senate Chamber, and make it the object of secret, confidential deliberation. Our own experience shows that, in this respect, there has been no improvement: the art of keeping state se-

[1] Exec. Jour., IV, 122, Committee Report. Clayton said in 1854 that the principles laid down in this report had since governed the action of the senate. By rule 40 of those adopted in 1868 and rule 73 of those adopted in 1877 it was provided that the votes of individuals should be secret, but that the fact of nomination, confirmation, or rejection should not be considered secret.

[2] Exec. Jour., VI, pp. 18-19.

[3] Congr. Record, 2d Sess., 44th Congr., p. 659, Rule 73.

crets is no better understood than it formerly was."[1] Nor did this art become better understood as time went on. In 1869, the New York *Times*, apropos of the publication of the Hale-Perry correspondence, said: "The fact that all the proceedings of the Senate in executive session are regularly disclosed and made public, would naturally suggest the absurdity of keeping up such a hollow sham any longer. It simply allows certain newspapers to trade on the lack of honor of certain senators."[2] Similar expressions may be found at almost any time, and the ease with which what is transacted in executive session at the present time becomes known, needs no example.

At first the honor of senators had been trusted to keep secret the executive proceedings, but a breach of the rules in 1844[3] by a senator who furnished to a newspaper, for publication, documents communicated in confidence to the senate, led to the enactment of a rule providing that: "Any officer or member of the Senate, convicted of disclosing for publication any written or printed matter directed by the Senate to be held in confidence, shall be liable, if an officer, to dismissal from the service of the Senate, and in the case of a member

[1] Congr. Deb., vol. VII, 2d Sess., 21st Congr., p. 294.

[2] New York Daily *Times*, April 21, 1869, p. 6.

[3] Two earlier breaches of the rules had been known to the senate. The first was committed by Senator Mason, who, when a sketch of the Jay treaty, upon which an injunction of secrecy had been imposed, was published by the *Aurora*, during the recess of congress, sent his copy of the treaty to the paper. This action was highly approved of by some senators and was taken no notice of officially by the senate. The other breach of the rules, which called forth a resolution of censure, was committed by General Pickering, who read in public session a confidential communication of the president; but, as it was several years after its receipt, and as it had in the meantime been published in a newspaper, the resolution of censure was thought by many to be undeserved. (Annals of Congr., 3d Sess., 11th Congr., pp. 67-83.)

to suffer expulsion from the body."[1] Later the rules provided for the infliction of the same penalty upon one revealing the "secret or confidential proceedings of the Senate."[2] No senator has ever been expelled under this rule and yet, as has been seen, the proceedings in executive session have, nevertheless, continued to be known.

This inability to keep secret what is done in executive sessions has been one of the arguments most frequently urged in favor of their abolition. Other objections made to them are that they are undemocratic, that they are an evasion of official duty and responsibility, and that the people have a right to know what is being done. Many, like Mr. Sherman, even consider the secret sessions unconstitutional, holding that the clause of the constitution authorizes secrecy only in particular cases, and not as a general rule. But perhaps the strongest argument against them is the opportunity thus offered for partizanship and corruption; and especially for the operation of the spoils system and that strange form of dictation which is the result of the so-called "Courtesy of the Senate," whose existence many think is, in the main, due to the privacy of executive sessions. The assertions frequently made by senators, as well as by others, that stories are told and things said in secret session which never would be in open session, tend to confirm this view. Occasionally, during the first half century of the government, proposals were made for the abolition of secrecy in executive sessions, and from about 1840 to 1868 such proposals were very frequent. After that little attention seems to have been paid to the matter until about 1885, since which time there has been much agitation of the subject and frequent proposals for a change made.

[1] Exec. Jour., VI, pp. 270, 273.

[2] Congr. Globe, 2d Ssss., 40th Congr., p. 1630, Rule 50.

## II. NOMINATIONS.

When the first nominations of the president came before the senate for concurrence, it was resolved that the consent of the senate should be given by ballot.[1] In the discussion, this method was objected to on the ground that it was beneath the dignity of the senate, which should be open, bold, and unawed by any consideration whatever, and because it would be productive of caballing and bargaining for votes. A few days later an attempt to reverse the decision failed; but, when an expression of Washington in favor of a *viva voce* vote had been secured,[2] this method was adopted by the senate.[3]

Washington's suggestions regarding the mode of communication to be observed between the president and senate were also adopted. The senate seems to have been in favor of oral communications.[4] To the committee appointed to confer with him on the subject Washington said:

"Oral communications may be proper, also, for discussing the propriety of sending representatives to foreign ports, and ascertaining the grade, or character, in which they are to appear, and may be so in other cases.

"With respect to nominations my present ideas are, that, as they point to a single object, unconnected in its nature with any other object, they had best be made by written message. In this case the acts of the President and the acts of Senate will stand upon clear, distinct and responsible grounds.

"Independently of this consideration, it would be no pleasing thing, I conceive, for the President, on the one hand, to be present and hear the propriety of his nomi-

[1] Exec. Jour., I, 7.

[2] Washington, Works, vol. XI, p. 415.

[3] Exec. Jour., vol. I, p. 19.

[4] Washington, Works, vol. XI, p. 415.

nations questioned; nor for the Senate, on the other hand, to be under the smallest restraint from his presence from the fullest and freest inquiry into the character of the persons nominated." [1]

He also suggested that the time, place, and manner of communication should be left to the president. The opinions of Washington having been reported to the senate, it was:

"*Resolved*, That when nominations shall be made in writing by the President of the United States to the Senate, a future day shall be assigned, unless the Senate unanimously direct otherwise, for taking them into consideration. That when the President of the United States shall meet the Senate in the Senate Chamber, the President of the Senate shall have a seat on the floor, be considered as the head of the Senate, and his chair shall be assigned to the President of the United States. That when the Senate shall be convened by the President of the United States, to any other place, the President of the Senate and the Senators shall attend at the place appointed. The Secretary of the Senate shall attend to take the minutes of the Senate. That all questions shall be put by the President of the Senate, either in the presence or absence of the President of the United States; and the Senators shall signify their assent or dissent, by answering *viva voce*, aye or no."[2]

Although provision is thus made for the president making his nominations in person and for the decision of the senate upon them in his presence, it does not appear that this method was ever adopted, even in the case of ambassadors, which Washington had thought might

[1] Washington, Works, XI, 418. He said further: "It is probable that the place may vary. . . . Whenever the government shall have buildings of its own, an executive chamber will no doubt be provided, where the Senate will generally attend the President."

[2] Exec. Jour., I, p. 19. This rule is still found among the senate rules.

be advisable. Had the other method been followed, the influence of the president would undoubtedly have been increased, and the independence of the senate decreased; so that it may well be doubted whether there would have grown up that freedom of dealing with the president's nominations which now makes it necessary for him, if he wishes his nominations confirmed, to first confer with and obtain the consent of the senators from the state for which the nomination is made.

In the early days of the senate, that part of the rule which provides that a nomination shall not be considered the same day that it is received was frequently set aside, the nomination being considered as soon as received; or, if it was laid upon the table for a few days, "when called up for consideration the members of the state interested in the appointment would give the Senate what information they might possess regarding the person nominated, occasionally other members would give their opinions, and, on these statements, the senators relied."[1] Ordinarily only when the person nominated was unknown or charges were made against him, or in case of nomination of one who had had charge of the disbursements of money, was the nomination referred to a committee. Sometimes also nominations of ministers were referred to the committee on foreign affairs to inquire regarding the expediency of the appointment.[2]

A proposal, made in 1822, to refer all nominations to the appropriate standing committee was tabled.[3] With the increasing number of nominations, the number of nominees regarding whom nothing was known naturally increased,

[1] Statement of Mr. Johnson. (Congr. Debates, 2d Sess., 20th Congr., p. 91.) The early senators also frequently consulted members of the other house regarding nominations. (Annals of Congr., 1st Sess., 10th Congr., p. 348.)

[2] Congr. Globe, 2d Sess., 20th Congr., p. 91.

[3] Exec. Jour., III, pp. 294, 297.

thus necessitating more frequent reference to committees; but it was not until 1868 that a rule was adopted requiring all nominations to be referred to the appropriate standing committee, unless otherwise ordered.[1] At the same time it was provided that a nomination should not be considered on the same day that it was reported by the committee, except by unanimous consent.

The need of communication between the president and senate, on nominations, soon appeared. The rejection by the senate of one of Washington's early nominations, led him to suggest that it might be expedient, in cases in which nominations seemed questionable to the senate, to communicate with him, that he might give his reasons for making the nomination under discussion.[2] In pursuance of this recommendation, it became customary, in case of doubt, to call directly by resolution upon the president or heads of departments for information or papers, or to refer the nomination to a committee to look into the matter. In one of the first cases the secretary of foreign affairs came into the senate by invitation, to give his information.[3] The committees often summoned the heads of the departments to appear before them, and sometimes even waited upon the president. The latter was done during the administrations of John Adams, Jefferson, and Madison; but the constitutionality of the practice was questioned both by Adams and by Madison; and, according to Mr. Sedgwick, the chairman of a committee which waited upon Adams in connection with the nomination of Vans Murray as minister plenipotentiary to France, and who himself confessed the proceeding to be "an infraction of correct principles," Adams refused to consent to an interview, until it was agreed that it should be strictly

[1] Congr. Globe, 2d Sess., 40th Congr., p. 1630, Rule 37.

[2] Annals of Congress, 1st Sess., 1st Congr., p. 61.

[3] Exec. Jour., I, 6, 7.

unofficial.[1] Madison went farther, and absolutely refused to confer with a committee specially authorized to call upon him,[2] sending to the senate a written communication in which he pointed out that the appointment of a committee to confer immediately with the executive lost sight of the coördinate relations of the senate and the executive.[3]

Besides this, there was then a great deal of informal communication and intercourse, though not as much as at present, both before and after nomination. Thus Adams writes: "Great pains have sometimes been taken by Senators, and Representatives too, to obtain nominations to offices, sometimes for themselves, sometimes for their favorites; sometimes with success and sometimes without;"[4] and Jefferson expressed surprise, when Short was rejected as minister, that his friends in the senate had not informed him of the intention, that he might have given his reasons for the nomination. The efforts of senators of a later day to influence nominations are too well known to need examples.

Of the agency of the senate in appointments, Hamilton had said: "It will be the office of the President to *nominate*, and with the advice and consent of the Senate to *appoint*. There will, of course, be no exertion of *choice* on the part of the Senators. They may defeat one *choice* of the Executive, and oblige him to make another; but they cannot themselves *choose*—they can only ratify or reject the choice of the President. They might even entertain a preference to some other person,

[1] Hamilton, Works, ed. by J. C. Hamilton, vol. VI, p 399.

[2] He refused to meet a committee to whom the nomination of Gallatin had been referred in the usual way, "to inquire and report to the Senate," but said that, if they were specially authorized by the senate, he would receive them; yet, when they were so authorized, he still refused to meet them. (Exec. Jour., II, pp. 353, 354.)

[3] Exec. Jour., II, p. 382.

[4] J. Adams, Works, VI, p. 535.

at the very moment they were assenting to the one proposed, because there might be no positive ground of opposition to him; and they could not be sure, if they withheld their assent, that the subsequent nomination would fall upon their own favorite, or upon any other person in their estimation more meritorious than the one rejected." [1]

Under Washington the senate, in the main, confined itself to such an exercise of its powers. The rejection of a nomination because of the hostility of the senators of the state for which the appointment was made; and their preference for another, met with a sharp rebuke from Washington.[2]

Though Washington demanded a careful consideration of his nominations, he wished to have the holders of office such as the senate wished, and in his nominations sought to choose those who would be agreeable to the senate. Thus, in 1794, when Gouverneur Morris, minister to France, was very unpopular with Republican senators, and this became known to Washington, he expressed informally a willingness to recall Mr. Morris, and appoint a person of the opposite party, if they would designate a fit person. Accordingly, the Democratic senators held a caucus in which they decided to recommend Burr. A committee, consisting of Madison, Monroe, and another, was appointed to wait on Washington and communicate their desires. Washington, however, refused to appoint Burr, saying that it had been a rule of his life never to appoint any one of whose integrity he was not assured; but that if they would designate a person in whom he could confide, he would nominate him. Another caucus was accordingly held at which it was unanimously resolved to adhere to

[1] Hamilton, Works, ed. by Ford, vol. IX. "Federalist," p. 416, No. LXVI.

[2] Exec. Jour., I, 16, 17.

the former decision. Washington then showed that, though desirous of pleasing senators, he would not suffer dictation, and, on the second meeting with the committee, and their insistence on their former choice, he told them that his decision was irrevocable. The committee still remained inflexible, and Washington finally appointed Monroe.[1]

With the accession of Adams to the presidency, there being a large Federalist majority in the senate, and Hamilton the real leader of the party, conditions were favorable for the senate to encroach on the power of the president. Adams wrote, in regard to this, that combinations and committees of senators were sent to him to remonstrate regarding nominations; and, if they could not prevail, obtained majorities in the senate against the nominations.[2] The change in the attitude of the senate from the preceding administration is shown by the fact that, though Adams had many less nominations to make than Washington, eight of his were rejected, and nine lost from being postponed to the last of the session, while but five of Washington's were rejected.

Under Jefferson, as under Adams, there was in the senate a large majority of the party of the president, but Jefferson, unlike Adams, being the real leader of his party, at first met with little opposition in his appointments, only three being rejected during the first six years. Toward the end of his administration, however, a disposition to control him in the exercise of this power appeared.[3] This was first shown in the rejection of Short as minister to Russia, which[4] indicated the termination of the individual personal influence of Jefferson and was the

[1] Life of Burr, I, 408, 409.

[2] Works, VI, 535. See also *Ibid.*, IX, 301, and Jefferson, Works, IV, 261.

[3] Statement of J. Q. Adams, found in Adams, Life of Gallatin, 389–390, and J. Adams, Works, IX, 302.

[4] According to J. Q. Adams.

forerunner of a more extensive plan for influencing nominations which began with the administration of Madison.

Under both Jefferson and Madison this dictation of the senate, unlike that under Adams, was effected by a small knot of senators operating mainly in secret session.[1] During Madison's first term nineteen nominations were rejected, and though, when the actions of these senators became known to the public, the prime movers lost their popularity and were compelled to retire from the senate, the seeds of usurpation of power by the senate were left behind. Thus far, however, this action of the senate had attracted so little attention that both Kent and Story, the one writing in 1832 and the other in 1833, take no notice of it. Story speaks of the senate as having "but a slight participation in the appointments to office,"[2] and Kent says: "Having no agency in the nomination, nothing but simply consent or refusal, the spirit of personal intrigue and personal attachment must be pretty much extinguished, for a want of means to gratify it."[3]

Though several of Jackson's nominations were rejected,[4] they were so bad that it is only strange that more were not. He also attempted to coerce the senate by renominations, a practice which was then new, though since followed to a considerable extent, especially by Tyler.

With the withdrawal of Jackson from the presidency, and the accession of a man who did not enjoy his great popularity, the senate was once more able

[1] Adams, Life of Gallatin, pp. 389-391.

[2] Commentaries, sec. 752.

[3] Commentaries, Lecture XIII, vol. I, p. 288.

[4] Niles' Register, vol. 46, July 12, 1834, p. 329: "It is stated that the Senate at the last session confirmed 449 nominations and rejected only 17."

to make its influence felt in nominations.[1] This influence was the result of a practice, followed from the first, of depending upon the senator from the state for which the nomination was made for information regarding it. After a time it came to be a fixed rule that a nomination would be rejected if the senator of the state concerned declared it to be unfit,[2] and finally on the mere ground that the nomination was personally obnoxious to him.[3]

With the full establishment of this practice all freedom of nomination naturally passed from the president to the various senators and members of congress, the president being compelled, if he wished his nominations confirmed, to first obtain the approval of the senators from the state in which the appointment was to be made.[4] The practice, which was checked somewhat by the popular disapproval of the action of Conkling and Platt in resigning their seats because the president refused to allow them to disburse the patronage of New York state, has since fully recovered its former strength, as is shown by the recent rejection of the nominations of Hornblower and Peckham.

The power of the senate in appointments has been increased in other ways. One of these is by the increase of the offices to which appointments are made with the concurrence of the senate. A very considerable increase

[1] Benton, Thirty Years' View, II, 629; and Congr. Deb., 2d Sess., 23d Congr., pp. 563, 564, where Mr. Hill says: "Some persons for a few years past, have seemed to manifest a longing desire that the Senate should have a hand in the management of the executive departments beyond the power the Senate possesses as a coördinate branch of the legislature."

[2] In case the senators belonged to the party of the president.

[3] Such a case is noted in the New York *Times* of 1869 (April 19, p. 4), the custom, which it says had prevailed to some extent before, being severely criticised.

[4] Senators and committees of the senate have acknowledged that such is the case.

was made when, in 1836, a law was passed providing for the appointment, with the advice and consent of the senate, of deputy postmasters in all the offices at which the commission allowed to the postmaster amounted to $1000.00 or upwards.[1] Moreover, owing to the great increase in the number of officials to be appointed, and the consequent impossibility of the president knowing the character of all, senators have obtained a great influence in the nomination to the lower offices for which their confirmation was not needed. In 1861, the nomination of all lower postmasters was unconditionally turned over to congressmen, by an official announcement that, thereafter, such nominations would be made on the recommendation of the members of congress of the different districts, and that applications addressed to them would receive attention earlier than if sent to the department, thus saving much delay and trouble.[2] In other departments, also, the influence of senators became paramount. In 1869, a senator said in debate: "It is an every day occurrence that applicants for office apply to Senators and Representatives assuring them that their recommendation alone is lacking to secure them the coveted position; and some of the departments, I am told, have actually kept a debit and credit account with members to show the number of appointments they are entitled to, and receive."[3]

The disbursement of the patronage came to occupy a third of the working time of senators[4] and led them to neglect their legislative duties, while tempting them to

[1] Statutes at Large, vol. V, p. 87, 1st Sess., 24th Congr., chap. 270, sec. 33.

[2] New York Semi-weekly *Tribune*, March 15, 1861.

[3] Congr. Globe, 2d Sess., 41st Congr., pp. 17, 18. In the 2d Sess., 42d Congress, it was said that Mr. Trumbull in fifteen months made 103 recommendations. This was, however, denied by Mr. Trumbull. (Congr. Globe, p. 1181.)

[4] Statement of Garfield during his presidency.

make the support of an administration dependent upon obtaining nominations for their friends. This usurpation of the appointing power, which, according to the report of the civil service commission of 1871, tended to make the president and his secretaries merely the appointment clerks of congress,[1] was one of the evils which the civil service reform sought to check.

The movement for civil service reform began in the senate with the introduction of a bill by Mr. Sumner in 1864;[2] and, from that time, the subject was occasionally brought up in both houses of congress, and urged by the presidents. The first step was taken in 1871, by the passage of a resolution authorizing the president to prescribe rules and regulations for the admission of persons into the civil service. It was proposed in the senate as an amendment to an appropriation bill, and passed without debate.[3] Under this act a commission was appointed by the president, which reported rules for the regulation of the civil service, that were at once put in operation. In 1872 and 1873 congress made appropriations for carrying these rules into effect; but, in spite of the success of the reform and the recommendations of the president, no appropriations were made after those years, and consequently the active work of the commission was suspended, though it was still left in existence. Thus the experiment failed through lack of the support of congress.

The most serious obstacle to an improvement was found to be the system by which the appointing power had been so largely encroached upon by congressmen;[4]

[1] 2d Sess., 42d Congr., Sen. Docs., No. 10, pp. 6, 7.

[2] Congr. Globe, 1st Sess., 38th Congr., p. 1985. The bill was never called up.

[3] *Ibid.*, 3d Sess., 41st Congr., p. 1997. This was regarded by the committee on the judiciary as only the first step in the reform. The bill was so introduced only because it was impossible otherwise to get the attention of congress for it.

[4] Annual message of President Hayes, 2d Sess., 46th Congr.

and the part of the system which had been the most unsatisfactory was that in which the senate had the greatest ability to thwart it, namely, in connection with those nominations which required their advice and consent.[1] The report of the civil service commission of 1874 pointed this out, and called attention to the fact that, in this regard, an effective reform could be brought about only when the senate and the executive should act upon the same general theory of conferring office;[2] and President Grant, recognizing the impracticability of rules in regard to such offices, unless sustained by the action of the senate, advised leaving this portion of the subject to the future.[3]

President Hayes repeatedly, but without effect, recommended legislation on the subject.[4] The death of Garfield by the hand of a disappointed office seeker brought home so vividly the evils of the then existing system as to induce congress, at the next session, in accordance with the recommendation of President Arthur, to again make an appropriation for the support of the civil service commission; and the following session a bill was passed establishing the commission, only five voting against it in the senate.[5]

This law affected only the departments in Washington, and post offices, and custom offices where over fifty were employed, leaving untouched all that class of officers whose confirmation belonged to the senate, and providing that no one whose confirmation belonged to the senate should be required to be classified or to pass an examination unless by the consent of the senate.[6] The

[1] 1st Sess., 43d Congr., Sen. Docs., No. 53, pp. 88, 89.

[2] *Ibid.*

[3] *Ibid.*

[4] Congr. Record, 2d Sess., 45th Congr., p. 4; 2d Sess., 46th Congr., p. 3; 3d Sess., 46th Congr.

[5] *Ibid.*, 2d Sess., 47th Congr., p. 661.

[6] Sec. 7 of the bill.

bill did not touch foreign ambassadors or officers of that class or lower postmasters, and yet it was declared that it would relieve senators of three-fourths of their troubles.[1]

To guard against the exercise of an improper influence upon the board of examiners it was provided that no recommendation of a senator or representative, except in regard to character, should be received or considered by any one concerned in making the examination.[2]

The support of the act has not been altogether satisfactory, and the large number of offices to which it does not apply still leaves much room for the interference of the senate. The number of offices to which the law applies has been constantly increased, however, so that, while in 1883 but eleven per cent.[3] came under its regulation, about twenty-five per cent. do now,[4] and efforts are constantly made to further extend it; while the frequent motions made to repeal the law have met with no success.[5]

When it is seen to what an extent the senate has encroached upon the power in appointments undeniably granted to the president, it is not surprising to find that it has also shown itself ready to interpret the constitution in its favor, whenever there is an opportunity. Such an opportunity is afforded by the clause which gives to the president power "to fill all Vacancies that may happen during the recess of the Senate, by granting Commissions which shall expire at the End of the next Session."

[1] Congr. Record, 47th Congr., 2d Sess., p. 244.

[2] *Ibid.*, p. 656.

[3] Ninth Annual Report of the Civil Service Commission, p. 10.

[4] *World* Almanac, 1895. This is more than half of the offices in importance and salary.

[5] The amendment of the constitution so as to give the election of certain officers to the people, or to create a house of electors to confirm or elect officers, were alternative reforms proposed. (Congr. Record, 1st Sess., 47th Congr., pp. 85, 3767.)

Washington, on the advice of Hamilton and Jay,[1] decided that this did not give him power to appoint to an original vacancy, during the recess of the senate.[2] John Adams[3] and Jefferson,[4] however, acted under the opposite interpretation, without being questioned by the senate; but, when a similar course was followed by Madison, a resolution protesting against it was introduced and debated, though not voted on.[5] A similar resolution of 1825 was laid upon the table by a majority of two, after a long debate, in the course of which each side declared that the previous practice supported its view.

While it was acknowledged that the president had a right at any time to appoint special agents, without the advice and consent of the senate, there was a difference of opinion as to what special agents were and the duties which could be assigned to them. In the second session of the Twenty-first Congress, when the appropriation for a treaty with the Ottoman Porte, negotiated by special agents, who of course were not nominated to the

[1] Hamilton's Works, ed. by Lodge, VIII, p. 407.

[2] The cases cited by the opponents of this theory, in which the practice of Washington seems to have been different, prove on examination not to apply exactly. Thus Mr. Short, when commissioned by Washington to adjust the boundary between Spain and the United States, was already resident minister in Madrid. The appointments to the Barbary States, without the consent of the senate, could be justified on the ground that the countries were in a state of war, and also because the senate had previously given its consent to the negotiation of a treaty; and Morris seems to have been appointed as a private agent rather than as a public minister. (Annals of Congr., 1st Sess., 13th Congr., pp. 751–753, and Congr. Deb., vol. II, part 1, 1st Sess., 19th Congr., pp. 609–614.)

[3] As shown by the appointment, without asking the advice of the senate, of his son, then minister to Berlin, to negotiate a treaty with Sweden; and of Rufus King to negotiate a treaty with Russia.

[4] Appointment of Short. See statement of Jefferson's position in his Works, vol. V, p. 360; for lists of precedents and discussion, Annals of Congr., 1st Sess., 13th Congr., pp. 704, 720, 721, 752; Congr. Deb., 1st Sess., 19th Congr., p. 614.

[5] Exec. Jour., II, 416.

senate, was agreed to; it was accompanied by a resolution stating that this should not be considered as "sanctioning, or in any way approving, the appointment of these persons, by the President alone, during the recess of the Senate, and without their advice and consent, as commissioners to negotiate a treaty with the Ottoman Porte."[1] There were, however, many who, like Madison, thought this the wrong interpretation of the constitution.[2] In 1863 a committee of the senate held that the power to make such appointments was necessary from the very nature of the treaty-making power;[3] and the presidents have continued to employ special agents for this purpose.

With regard to original vacancies in statutory offices, those who denied the right of the president to fill them in the recess of the senate, did so not only on the ground that a vacancy can not happen in an office not before filled, but also because, in the case of an office created by the legislature, the vacancy would necessarily exist prior to the recess, and, therefore, could not be said to happen in the recess. Some, while denying the first, admitted the second, while others interpreted "vacancy happening in the recess" as a vacancy happening to exist in the recess.

The early congresses seem to have held that the president had not a right to appoint to an original statutory vacancy, for, when a law creating new offices was passed so near the end of the session as not to give time for filling them, the president would be specially authorized to do so during the recess.[4] Moreover, Mr. Gore said, in 1814, that this was the invariable practice;[5] and in 1826

[1] Congr. Debates, 2d Sess., 21st Congr., p. 310, yeas 25, nays 18.

[2] Madison, Works, IV, 369; III, 268.

[3] 3d Sess., 37th Congr., Sen. Reports, No. 80, p. 8.

[4] Statutes at Large, vol. 1, p. 200, 3d Sess., 1st Congr., chap. 15, sec. 4.

[5] Annals of Congress, 1st Sess., 13th Congr., p. 656.

Mr. Tazewell said that it had never been pretended by any one, at any time, that the president might make an appointment to an original statutory vacancy.[1] In 1831 he said, further, that but one president had ever attempted to make such appointments, and that, in that case, the nominations were rejected by the senate, and a report made setting forth the constitutional construction, to which the executive afterwards assented.[2]

This view was upheld by Attorney General Mason in 1845,[3] but the report of a committee of the Thirty-seventh Congress shows that appointments were, nevertheless, occasionally made to original statutory vacancies in the recess of the senate;[4] and, in 1868, Attorney General Evarts held that this, and the case of a vacancy happening in an office during the session of congress, were exactly the same, and that in both cases the president had a right to make an appointment during the recess.[5] After that it seems to have been usual for the president, during the recess, to make appointments to original vacancies if they happened to occur, though congress still occasionally specially authorized the president to make such appointments,[6] thus apparently not recognizing that he had a right to do so in any case. The claim was also frequently disputed in the senate, and in the Thirty-seventh,[7] Fiftieth,[8] and Fifty-first[9] Congresses, committees were appointed to look into the matter.

As the early congresses had held that the president

[1] Congr. Debates, vol. II, part i, 1st Sess., 19th Congr., p. 607.

[2] Congr. Debates, vol. VII, 2d Sess., 23d Congr., p. 225.

[3] 4 Opinions, 363.

[4] 3d Sess., 37th Congr., Sen. Reports, No. 80, pp. 9, 11.

[5] 12 Opinions, 457.

[6] Congr. Globe, 2d Sess., 39th Congr., pp. 407–409. Also, 3d Sess., 37th Congr., Sen. Reports, No. 80, p. 9.

[7] 3d Sess., Sen. Reports, No. 80.

[8] 1st Sess.

[9] 1st Sess.

could not appoint to an original vacancy, so it would seem that they also held that he could not fill vacancies happening during the previous session; for, on one occasion at least, an act was passed specially authorizing the president to make such appointments during the recess,[1] and Madison thought himself unable to make an appointment to fill a vacancy which had existed since the last session.[2] With Monroe a different practice was introduced,[3] and was followed by most of the subsequent presidents,[4] who were supported in it by the opinions of the attorney generals.[5] During Lincoln's administration, however, it would seem that a different view prevailed, for in the Washington despatches of the New York *Times* for March 9, 1861, the following appears: "Mr. Lincoln found about seventy vacancies in appointments under government. These must be filled while the Senate is in session, or cannot be until Congress meets again."

It has always been the practice of the president to fill vacancies created during the recess by removals though a minority have held that they could not be considered to have happened.

Another way in which the senate, when in opposition to the president, has curtailed his power, is by refusing to act upon his nominations at the end of his term. This was done at the end of the term of J. Q. Adams, when the senate refused to act on his nominations for associate justices of the supreme court, on the ground

[1] Statutes at Large, vol. I, p. 749, 3d Sess., 5th Congr., chap. 47.

[2] Madison, Works, vol. III, p. 400.

[3] 3d Sess., 37th Congr., Sen. Reports, No. 80.

[4] *Ibid.*, pp. 9-12; Congr. Record, 1st Sess., 51st Congr., p. 176.

[5] Digest of Opinions of Attorney Generals, in House Misc. Docs., 2d Sess., 48th Congr., No. 15, pp. 288-294, §§ 3, 13, 34, 35, 59, 66, 78, 79, 88, 89; and Opinions of Attorney Generals, vol. 17, p. 521. There was one exception, Attorney General Mason, in 1845, holding the opposite. (4 Op., 363.)

that the people having in an election expressed their disapprobation of the existing president, he should make only such nominations as were actually necessary to carry on the government. Under Tyler this was carried further, it being informally agreed, toward the end of his term, not to act on any of his nominations.

In the early days of the government the custom, which has now become fixed, of confirming without question or reference all cabinet nominations, was not firmly established, though greater deference has always been paid to these nominations of the president than to any others,[1] and they have, in general, been accepted without a dissenting voice.[2] The fear of a rejection, however, prevented Jefferson nominating Gallatin as secretary of the treasury, to the old congress, which was strongly Federalist;[3] and Madison, being threatened with a rejection of Monroe if he were nominated as secretary of foreign affairs, gave up his wishes and nominated Robert Smith, who was suggested to him by certain senators;[4] while later, when Monroe was nominated as secretary of foreign affairs, an attempt was made to find a reason for his rejection by an examination of his accounts.[5] Moreover, three cabinet nominations have

[1] No vote is recorded against any of the cabinet nominations of Washington, Jefferson, Van Buren, Taylor, Fillmore, or Pierce, and votes are recorded against only one each of the cabinet nominations of J. Adams, J. Q. Adams, Monroe and Buchanan, while votes are recorded against four of Madison's nominations, and against two of both Lincoln's and Johnson's.

[2] In the 2d Sess., 39th Congr. (Congr. Globe, p. 384), Mr. Fessenden said: "It has always been considered, since the foundation of the government, as a matter of course, as a general rule—there may have been one or two exceptions, and I think there have been—that the President might select such persons as he pleased to be members of his cabinet—the general idea of the Senate has been, whether they liked the men or not, to confirm them without difficulty."

[3] Stevens, Gallatin, p. 185.

[4] Adams, Life of Gallatin, p. 390.

[5] Exec. Jour., II, p. 188.

actually been rejected, each one, however, under unusual circumstances.[1] Now, nominations for the cabinet, like those of senators for office, are confirmed at once, and without reference.

The omission in the constitution of a provision regarding removals, placed that subject among those which must be decided by inference, thus giving an opportunity for opposing views. The question came up for decision in the very first congress assembled under the new constitution, being caused by a clause in the bill for the organization of the departments, which provided that the heads of the departments should be appointed "by the President, by and with the advice and consent of the Senate, and be removable by the President."[2]

Starting from this the discussion extended to the subject of removals in general. Four different opinions were advanced. There were a considerable number who held that no removal could be made but by impeachment, and much of the discussion in the house went to the upholding or refuting of this; which, however justifiable as an interpretation of the constitution, should, it would seem, have been ruled out from the first on account of its impracticability, even with the small number of offices then needed. A second party held that, since the constitution was silent regarding removals, the legislature might give the power to whom it would; while a third, regarding the power of removal as incident to that of appointment, held, therefore, that it was vested in the president and senate.[3] Still another party maintained that, inasmuch as the power of removal was an executive power, it belonged to the president; and this

[1] Roger B. Taney (Exec. Jour., IV, p. 427, yeas 18 nays 28); James M. Porter (Exec. Jour., VI, p. 227, yeas 3, nays 38); and David Henshaw (Exec. Jour., VI, pp. 210, 211, yeas 8, nays 34).

[2] Annals of Congress, 1st Sess., 1st Congr., p. 385.

[3] This is the opinion held by the supreme court, 13 Ott. Rep., 227, 237; 13 Peters Rep., 259, 261, *Ex parte* Hennen.

was the view which finally prevailed, being adopted in the house by a considerable majority.[1]

In the senate the subject was debated four days, the discussion being mainly as to whether the senate was or was not associated with the president in removals. Mr. Ellsworth, whose opinion as a member of the convention carries weight, says: "There is an explicit grant of power to the President which contains the power of removal. The executive power is granted, not the executive powers hereinafter enumerated and explained. The President not the Senate, appoints, they only consent and advise. The Senate is not an executive council; has no executive power."[2] So equally divided was the senate on this subject, that it was only by the casting vote of the vice president that the clause, as adopted by the house, was retained.[3]

Under the first six presidents, with the exception of Jefferson, there was little or no abuse of the power of removal, and the subject seems to have attracted no attention until the action of Jackson brought it forcibly before the people.

The bill passed May fifteenth, 1820, limiting the tenure of office of certain officials to four years, by which the senate was enabled, through its power of confirmation, practically to remove all such officers at the end of four years, was ostensibly introduced only for the purpose of obtaining greater security for the upright performance of their duties by the officers concerned. Mr. Adams, however, said that the object of the law, which was drawn by Crawford, was to gain support for

[1] The clause as first adopted in the house implied a legislative grant of the power, and, attention being called to this, the language was changed. (Annals of Congress, 1st Sess., 1st Congr., pp. 399, 600-604.)

[2] J. Adams, Works, III, pp. 408, 412.

[3] Half of the members of the senate at that time had been members of the convention.

Crawford for the presidency.[1] Introduced in the senate, the bill passed its various stages in both houses without debate, and, in the senate, was ordered to a third reading by a vote of 29 to 4.[2] The tendency of this law did not, however, escape the attention of the statesmen of the time. Madison questioned its constitutionality,[3] and Jefferson, foreseeing clearly its effect, declared it to be more baneful than the unsuccessful attempt, at the beginning of the government, to make all officers irremovable, except with the consent of the senate.[4]

The first two presidents after the passage of the act, despite the urgency of senators, did not take advantage of the opportunities thus offered them, and renominated, at the expiration of office, everyone against whom there was no complaint.[5] Under their successors, however, the expiration of the four years' term came to be considered as the vacation of the office,[6] so that J. Q. Adams wrote in 1828: "The result of the act has been to increase the power of patronage exercised by the President, and still more that of the Senate and of every individual Senator."[7] So far reaching were the effects of the law that Calhoun said in 1846 that "it had done more toward making a revolution in the United States than almost any other law."[8]

A bill, introduced in 1826, for the repeal of this law and the substitution of one requiring a report at the end of every four years from all officers having charge of the collection or disbursement of the revenue, and providing for the removal of defaulters, was not voted on;[9] but in

[1] J. Q. Adams, Works, VII, 424.

[2] Annals of Congress, 1st Sess., 16th Congr., p. 674.

[3] Works, III, 200.

[4] Jefferson, Works, VII, 190.

[5] J. Q. Adams, Works, VI, 520, 521.

[6] Benton, Thirty Years' View, I, 82.

[7] J. Q. Adams, Works, VII, 425.

[8] Congr. Globe, 1st Sess., 29th Congr., p. 819.

[9] *Ibid.*, vol. II, part ii, 1st Sess., 19th Congr., App. p. 138.

1835 the same bill was introduced in the senate and passed by a vote of 31 to 16,[1] but was not acted upon in the house. Again in 1846 the senate repealed so much of the act as limited the tenure of office of paymasters to four years,[2] but the house disagreed to it, and the law still remains in full force, though an attempt has recently been made, in connection with the civil service reform, to repeal this and other laws limiting the tenure of office.

Another means by which it has been attempted to gain indirectly the power of removal, which the first senate, by the casting vote of the vice president, declared that it did not possess, was by calling upon the president to state his reasons for a removal, when acting upon the nomination to fill the vacancy so occasioned. Prior to 1826 there was no attempt to make this a general rule, but in individual cases unsuccessful resolutions of this character had been introduced.[3]

The bill proposed by the committee appointed in 1826 to consider the expediency of reducing the executive patronage, required the president, in making a nomination to fill a vacancy caused by a removal, to give his reasons for such removal, and was intended, according to Mr. Benton, "to operate as a restraint upon removals without cause and to make legal and general what the Senate itself and the members of the committees individually had constantly refused to do in isolated cases. It was," said he, "the recognition of a principle essential to the proper exercise of the appointing power, and entirely consonant to Mr. Jefferson's idea of removals; but never admitted

[1] Congr. Globe, vol. XI, part i, 2d Sess., 23d Congr., p. 576.

[2] *Ibid.*, 1st Sess., 29th Congr., pp. 833, 834.

[3] Benton, Thirty Years' View, I, 82. Congr. Debates, vol. VII, part i, p. 370. Exec. Jour., II, 504.

by any administration, nor enforced by the Senate against anyone—always waiting the legal enactment."[1]

This bill never coming before the senate for action, individual motions to inquire into the cause of certain removals continued to be made,[2] though for some time unsuccessfully. The majority held not only that the president had a right to remove all federal officers, but that the senate had no right to inquire into the cause of the removal, its[3] duty being confined to deciding regarding the fitness of the person nominated to fill the vacancy created, and the only remedy, in case of an abuse of power by the president, being impeachment. The senate in the past had not acted upon such a narrow interpretation but, on several occasions, had asserted its right to look behind the fitness of candidates, and upheld it by the rejection of the candidates, as in the case of Monroe's military nominations in 1822, and the cases of rejection of ministers because a mission, was not deemed expedient at the time the nomination was made.

Among the minority, at this time, were found various shades of opinion. While the most extreme held that the consent of the senate was as necessary for removals as for appointments, there were others who held that the president had a right to suspend an officer, but that if the person nominated as a successor was rejected then the former incumbent still remained in office;[4] while still others claimed for the senate only the right to restrain the president in the abuse of the power of removal.[5]

In 1835 a resolution was finally adopted in the senate, but not considered in the house, requiring the president to give his reasons for removals, in making nominations to fill the vacancies so occasioned. At the same time,

[1] Benton, Thirty Years' View, I, 82.
[2] Exec. Jour., IV, 70, 76.
[3] Congr. Deb., 1st Sess., 21st Congr., p. 457.
[4] J. Q. Adams, Works, VIII, p. 189.
[5] Congr. Debates, 1st Sess., 21st Congr., p. 385.

as has been said, the repeal of the tenure of office bill of 1820 was agreed upon by the senate.[1] During the same session of congress the senate had asserted its right, in an individual instance, to call upon the president for the reasons of a removal, stating, in the preamble of the resolution asking them, that they were requested because they might contain information necessary in the action of the senate on the nomination of a successor.[2] President Jackson refused to comply with the request, which he characterized as an "encroachment on the rights of the executive,"[3] and the senate upheld its view by the rejection of the nomination of a successor[4] and a second rejection on the renomination of the same person.[5]

This seems to be the only case prior to 1867 in which such a resolution was adopted. Similar ones during the administrations of Tyler[6] and Taylor[7] failed, many, however, voting against them who would have been in favor of a general rule on the subject, or of depriving the president altogether of the power.

In 1844 a committee on retrenchment reported against the power of removal in the president, and advised the passage of a law specifying "the disqualifications or reasons which will be considered in law sufficient to authorize removals."[8] A little later a motion to require the advice and consent of the senate in reducing the army at the end of the war failed, though several voted against it, not because they disapproved of the

[1] Congr. Debates, vol. XI, part i, 2d Sess., 23d Congr., p. 576.

[2] Exec. Jour., IV, pp. 465, 466.

[3] *Ibid.*, p. 468. He held that "the President, in cases of this nature, possesses the exclusive power of removal from office."

[4] *Ibid.*, p. 481.

[5] *Ibid.*, pp. 519, 528, 529.

[6] Exec. Jour., V, p. 401.

[7] Congr. Globe, 1st Sess., 31st Congr., pp. 74, 160.

[8] 1st Sess., 28th Congr., Sen. Docs., No. 399.

principle, but because they thought it unwise to decide so momentous a question without thorough debate.[1]

From this time till the close of the civil war, the slavery question, and then the conduct of the war, nearly banished all other questions. The system of partisan removals seems to have been accepted as a necessary evil, in the case of the senate, partly perhaps, because of the increasing share in the patronage which it had obtained.

The quarrel of congress with President Johnson caused it to seek every means of limiting his power and led to the passage of the tenure of office act of 1867. During the first session of the Thirty-ninth Congress both houses had been vehemently importuned to take from the president the power of removal.[2] The action of the president in renominating, during the recess, persons whom the senate in the preceding session had rejected—thus practically doing away with the senate's power of confirmation—as well as his removals from office and the general opposition to him, ensured the passage of the act at the next session.[3]

The bill, as first reported by the joint select committee on retrenchment and as adopted in the senate, provided that all officers appointed by and with the advice and consent of the senate, with the exception of the cabinet officers, should hold office until a successor had been duly appointed; except that, in the recess of the senate, the president might suspend an officer who had

[1] Congr. Globe, 1st Sess., 29th Congr., p. 959.

[2] *Ibid.*, 2d Sess., 39th Congr., p. 1517, statement of Mr. Howe.

[3] Mr. Edmunds, the chairman of the committee, however, in reporting the bill, said that he did so in no partisan spirit, and that he thought the bill one that would be good for any administration and all times; and it was frequently asserted in the debates that the action desired was not on account of partisan spirit or hatred of the president.

become "legally disqualified or incapable" to perform his duties; but this fact must be communicated to the senate for approval or disapproval within thirty days after its reassembling, and, if the senate did not concur in the suspension, the officer was to be restored. Furthermore, it guarded against the continued recommissioning of an officer by the president, without asking the consent of the senate, by providing that a vacancy, lawfully happening during the recess, might be filled by the president, the person appointed holding office till the end of the next session; when, if no appointment had been made with the advice and consent of the senate, the office should remain vacant until such an appointment could be made.[1]

In the debate, the subject was considered in all its bearings. The old question of the right of the president to make any removals was discussed, and the precedents for it enumerated; but the point which excited most discussion was the exception of the heads of the departments. The amendment proposed for striking out the clause in which this exception was made was twice voted down in the senate, the second time by a vote of 27 to 13.[2] In the house, a similar motion was first lost by two votes, but on reconsideration was adopted 75 to 66.[3] The senate refused to accede to this amendment, but a report of a conference committee was finally accepted, which adopted the house amendment with an amendment providing that the members of the cabinet should hold their offices respectively for and during the term of the president by whom they were appointed, and for one month thereafter, subject to removal by and with the advice and consent of the senate.[4] The bill

[1] Congr. Globe, 2d Sess., 39th Congr., p. 382.

[2] *Ibid.*, p. 548.

[3] *Ibid.*, pp. 944, 969.

[4] *Ibid.*, p. 1514.

thus amended was adopted in the senate by a vote of 22 to 10, and, being vetoed by President Johnson on the ground of its unconstitutionality,[1] was passed over the veto without debate.[2]

Considering the opinions expressed in the senate, during the debate on the bill, against compelling the president to retain unwelcome cabinet officers, and the holding of such views by a majority of the senate, as shown by their votes; their action in refusing to concur in the removal of Mr. Stanton from the office of secretary of war can only be accounted for by the personal quarrel with the president, and, therefore, too much importance should not be attached to this interpretation of the law by them. Their action on this subject, as well as the later repeal of the law and the remarks then made, discredit their earlier statements that, in passing the law, they were influenced only by general views regarding its expediency and constitutionality.

The denial by Mr. Stanton of the right of the president to suspend him from office under the constitution and laws of the United States, without the consent of the senate, is also remarkable, inasmuch as when the law was before the cabinet he was loudest in declaring it to be unconstitutional; and because it seemed to be taken for granted that the law would not apply to members of the cabinet appointed by Mr. Lincoln.[3]

Mr. Stanton was suspended from office during the recess of the senate, and when, on the assembling of congress, President Johnson notified the senate of his action, it refused, by a vote of 31 to 8, to concur in the suspension.[4] About a month thereafter the president removed Mr. Stanton, stating in his message to the senate an-

[1] Congr. Globe, 2d Sess., 39th Congr., p. 1964.

[2] *Ibid.*, p. 1966.

[3] Exec. Jour., vol. 16, p. 99.

[4] *Ibid.*, p. 129.

nouncing it, that he had done so in the exercise of the power and authority vested in him as president.[1] The senate at once passed a resolution declaring the act to be unconstitutional,[2] and the president, in his reply, upheld it on the ground that Mr. Stanton was appointed by his predecessor. After the trial of the president on impeachment, which followed in consequence of this act, and his acquittal, President Johnson nominated a successor to Mr. Stanton whom the senate confirmed, stating, however, that they considered the former incumbent illegally removed, but as he had relinquished his place they agreed to the appointment of a successor.[3]

In the second session of the Fortieth Congress, while the Stanton case was before the senate, a bill was reported as an addition to the tenure of office act, discussed, and passed in the senate, which further limited the executive power by forbidding the appointment by the president of most of the general and special agents before allowed, and by requiring the confirmation of the senate in the appointment of officers who before had been appointed by the president or his secretaries. The avowed purpose of this act was to decrease the expenses of the government. The bill passed the senate by a large majority.[4] In the house it was referred to a committee, and not called up.

At the third session of the Fortieth Congress a bill for the repeal of the tenure of office act was hurried through the house, under the previous question, without debate, and passed by a vote of 121 to 47.[5] In the senate a substitute was reported by the committee which, instead of repealing the act, provided for its amendment so as to except cabinet officers and not to require the

[1] Exec. Jour., vol. 16, p. 170.

[2] *Ibid.*, p. 172.

[3] *Ibid.*, pp. 236, 238, 239.

[4] Congr. Globe, 2d Sess., 40th Congr., p. 1037.

[5] *Ibid.*, 3d Sess., 40th Congr., p. 283.

president to give his reasons for suspension. This was discussed on two different days and the senate then refused to take it up.

At the next congress the repeal was again passed in the house without debate and sent to the senate. Meanwhile a bill to repeal the act had been introduced in the senate and indefinitely postponed, and one to amend the bill had been referred to a committee. On receipt of the house bill this was taken up. An attempt to pass it in the senate, without reference or discussion, failed, and it was amended so as to provide for the repeal of the first and second sections of the act and the substitution of a section which required the consent of the senate for the removal, during the session of congress, of an officer appointed by and with its consent; giving to the president, however, the right to suspend an officer during vacation. Such a suspension had to be reported to the senate within thirty days after its assembling, and a person nominated to the office thus left vacant. If the senate refused to consent to the nomination so made, and also to the suspension, then the suspended officer was entitled to resume his office.[1]

According to the interpretation of this given in the house during the discussion of the report, its essential difference from the original law lay in the fact that, under the law of 1867, the reasons for which the officer was suspended must be given, while according to the law proposed by the senate this was not necessary. The house refused to agree to the senate amendment, and the bill went to a committee of conference where it was further amended by striking out the portion regarding the result of the refusal of the senate to agree to a suspension, and inserting: "Then, and not otherwise, the President shall nominate another person as soon as practicable to said session of the Senate." The effect

[1] Congr. Globe, 1st Sess., 41st Congr., p. 246.

of this amendment, according to those who explained it in the house, was "to leave to the President, under the limitation of law, all the power that was ever claimed for the President under the Constitution of the United States, the suspension under the bill amounting practically to a removal." With this understanding the bill was agreed to in the house. In the house it had also been held that, if at the end of the session no person had been confirmed to fill a vacancy created by a suspension, the office would remain vacant; but in the senate it was maintained that the removed officer would again take his place. The interpretation of the senate was upheld by the attorney general, and was the one which prevailed. Practically, however, it made no difference, for the president could again suspend the officer removed upon his reinstatement in his office.

President Grant was not satisfied with this, and in his first annual message he recommended the repeal of the law, declaring it to be "inconsistent with a faithful and efficient administration of the government." Twice the repeal was passed in the house, and not acted on in the senate.[1] In the third session of the Forty-sixth, Congress, President Hayes, while speaking of civil service reform, urged its repeal;[2] and in 1877 Garfield, in advocating the repeal, said: "The President can remove no officer without the consent of the Senate, not often given unless the appointment of the successor is agreeable to the Senator in whose state the appointee resides."[3]

In the first session of both the Forty-eighth and Forty-ninth Congresses, a bill for the repeal of the law was again introduced in the house; and, in the first session of the Forty-ninth Congress, there was a long discussion

[1] 1st and 2d Sessions of the 42d Congress.

[2] Congr. Record, p. 3.

[3] Taken from Eaton, Secret Sessions, p. 41.

of the subject in the senate, brought on by the refusal of the attorney general, under the direction of President Cleveland, to comply with a resolution of the senate calling for "copies of all papers and documents that have been filed in the Department of Justice, since the first day of January, 1885, in relation to the management and conduct of the office of the district attorney of the United States of the Southern District of Alabama;"[1] the senate having under consideration the nomination of a person to take the place of the one suspended.

In the majority report of the committee of the judiciary, to whom the message was referred, it was stated that, since the passage of the act of March second, 1867, it had always been the practice of the committee of the judiciary, whenever a nomination was made proposing the removal from office of one person and the appointment of another, to address a note to the head of the department having such matter in charge, usually the attorney general; asking that all papers and information in the possession of the department, touching the conduct and character of the officer proposed to be removed, and of the person to be appointed, be sent to the committee for its information. This practice had been followed throughout all administrations with the unanimous approval of all the members of the committees, although the composition of the committees had been sometimes of one political character and sometimes of another.[2] When, in the present instance, there was delay in sending the information, a resolution passed the senate, without division, calling for such information. The senate declared the action of the attorney general to be "in violation of his official duty and subversive of the fundamental principles of the government and of a good administration thereof," and that consequently it

[1] Congr. Record, 1st Sess., 49th Congr., p. 1585.

[2] *Ibid.*

was their duty to refuse the confirmation of a successor to the officer removed.[1]

The papers were refused on the ground that they were private, but at the same time the president said: "I am also led unequivocally to dispute the right of the Senate, by the aid of any documents whatever or in any way, except through the judicial process of trial by impeachment, to review or revise the acts of the Executive, in the suspension, during the recess of the Senate, of the Federal Officials."[2]

It had frequently been asserted that, since its amendment, the tenure of office act had had no practical effect. This would certainly be the case if Cleveland's interpretation were to prevail, and, at the next session, a resolution for its repeal was introduced in the senate, and passed by a considerable majority.

### III. TREATIES.

Though treaties were regarded as part of the executive duties of the senate and, therefore, even after 1794, still considered in secret, there was no general rule forbidding disclosures concerning them until December 22, 1800. It is evident that, previously, they were not considered secret, since, when it was deemed expedient to keep secret the Jay treaty, a special order was passed placing it under the injunction of secrecy.[3] This rule, which provided "That all treaties which may hereafter be laid before the Senate shall also be kept secret until the Senate shall, by their resolution, take off the injunction of secrecy,"[4] was interpreted as extending the injunction of secrecy to all the proceedings of the senate, including the fact that a treaty had been

[1] Congr. Record, 1st Sess., 49th Congr., pp. 1587, 2810, 2814.

[2] *Ibid.*, p. 1903.

[3] Exec. Jour., I, 178.

[4] *Ibid.*, p. 361.

submitted to the senate, and its provisions.[1] In 1868 the rule was made more definite by providing that "all remarks and proceedings thereon, shall be kept secret," and in 1877 votes were included in the enumeration.[2]

The efficacy of these rules regarding treaties has been no greater than similar ones regarding nominations. The very first time an injunction of secrecy was imposed it was violated, and, in 1846, it was said in the senate that secret sessions on treaties amounted to nothing, since, whenever treaties were of sufficient importance to attract attention, they became known just as well as if considered in public.[3] This was one of the reasons urged in the frequent proposals for the abolition of secret sessions, in consideration of all or certain classes of treaties. In 1870 it was agreed that, thereafter, Indian treaties should be considered in open session, except when transmitted by the executive to the senate for its confidential consideration.[4]

The first treaty to be considered in open session, though proposals for such a course had often been made before in special cases, was the fisheries treaty with England. This innovation was due to the fact that the treaty was made a campaign issue, and neither party dared to risk the inference which might be drawn from their refusal to discuss it in public.

The expectations of Washington, and probably of the first senate also,[5] regarding the manner of procedure and the relation of the president and senate in the formation and consideration of treaties, have not been realized; it being apparent, even during the First Congress, that they would not be fully carried out.

[1] Exec. Jour., IV, 123, Report of Committee of 1830.

[2] Congr. Record, 2d Sess., 40th Congr., p. 1630, Rule 39; and 2d Sess., 44th Congr., p. 1877, Rule 67.

[3] Congr. Globe, 1st Sess., 29th Congr., p. 988.

[4] *Ibid.*, 2d Sess., 41st Congr., p. 1099.

[5] It seems to have acquiesced in his view.

Washington, when waited upon to ascertain his opinions regarding the mode of communication which should be observed between the president and senate on nominations and treaties, said. "In all matters respecting *treaties* oral communications seem indispensably necessary; because in these a variety of matters are contained, all of which not only require consideration, but some of them may undergo discussion, to do which by written communication would be tedious without being satisfactory."[1] Recognizing that different circumstances might require different means of communication and that the opinion of both the president and the senate regarding the best mode might change, he suggested that the rules of the senate should be accommodated to either oral or written communications, and this was accordingly done;[2] the senate thereby indicating their concurrence with the ideas of Washington and their expectation of holding personal communication with him.

It seems to have been expected that treaties would be gone over clause by clause, and modelled, by the president and senate together,[3] this being the course pursued in the formation of the first treaty. On August 21, 1789, Washington sent a message to the senate informing them that, on the next day, he would meet them in the senate chamber to discuss concerning the terms of an Indian treaty. As this is the only instance in which such a course was pursued, and as Washington evidently expected that the usual mode of communication on treaties would be oral, it seems worth while to give a portion of the interview, an account of which is found in Maclay's Journal, that the reason for the discontinuation of the practice may thus, if possible, be discovered.

[1] Washington, Works, vol. XI, p. 417.

[2] The rule still remains the same.

[3] J. Adams, Works, III, 409, statement of Mr. Butler in a senate debate.

At the appointed time Washington appeared in the senate, accompanied by General Knox; and, having stated the reason for his coming and that he had brought General Knox because he was well acquainted with the affair, a paper which he had brought with him, containing an account of the relations with the Indians and having annexed to it seven questions, was read, after which the vice president read the first question and put it to vote. As no one moved, Mr. Maclay tells us that, after a pause, and just as the vice president was about to put the question, he rose, and, speaking of the importance of the treaty and the lack of information, asked for the reading of the treaties and other documents mentioned in the paper. At this, he says: "I cast an eye at the President of the United States. I saw he wore an aspect of stern displeasure." There seemed evident reluctance to proceed. The first and second articles were postponed and then a commitment was proposed. Objections were made to this. It was said: "We were acting as a council. No council ever committed anything." Mr. Maclay spoke in favor of a commitment, and "as I sat down," he writes, "the President of the United States started up in a violent fret. 'This defeats every purpose of my coming here,' were the first words that he said. He then went on that he had brought his Secretary of War with him to give every necessary information; that the Secretary knew all about the business, and yet he was delayed and could not go on with the matter. He cooled, however, by degrees. Said he had no objection to putting off this matter until Monday, but declared he did not understand the commitment."

The president withdrew soon after, Mr. Maclay says, "with a discontented air;" and he writes further, "I can not now be mistaken. The President wishes to tread on the necks of the Senate. Commitment will bring the matter to discussion, at least in the committee, where he is not present. He wishes us to see with the eyes and hear with the ears of his Secretary only." When Washington attended on the next day the different points were taken up, debated, and decided without further misunderstanding.[1]

That Washington wished to "tread on the necks of the Senate," as Mr. Maclay suggested, but found himself unable to do so and therefore discontinued the practice of oral communications, does not accord with his character or treatment of the senate. It is more probable that the practice was discontinued because Washington saw that it restrained the freedom of debate; and, perhaps, as he suggested in the case of nominations, he found it unpleasant to have his propositions discussed and criticised in his presence.

Though giving up oral communications with the senate regarding treaties, he still continued, in most cases, to take the advice of the senate previous to the negotiation of a treaty.[2] His failure to do so in the negotiation of the treaty with Great Britain was held by some to be a violation of the constitution, but by others to be perfectly proper.[3]

On Indian treaties there was a question as to whether

[1] Journal of Maclay, pp. 128–133.

[2] In the negotiations with Spain, he asked the senate if they would consent to the extension of the powers of the minister lately appointed to that court, and would ratify a treaty made in conformity to those instructions (Exec. Jour., I, 106). In the negotiations with Algiers, he asked the senate if they would agree to a treaty of a certain form (Exec. Jour., I, 122); and before taking steps relative to the settling of the boundary between Nova Scotia and Maine, the senate was consulted. In regard to Indian treaties, it had been the unanimous opinion of his cabinet that a previous consultation of the senate was not necessary. Washington, nevertheless, frequently consulted the senate regarding such treaties (Exec. Jour., I, 21, 36, 55, 60, 88, 98).

[3] Williams, Statesman's Manual, I, p. 88; Life and Letters of Cabot, pp. 241, 243.

the final ratification of the government was necessary, or if the signature of the treaty by the negotiator should be considered binding, as had been the previous practice. Washington favored the first plan. A committee of the senate, to whom the question was referred on the receipt of the first Indian treaty, reported in favor of the old practice; but the report was set aside by the senate and the treaty submitted, ratified in due form.[1]

Adams, who disapproved of the executive powers entrusted to the senate, would naturally be inclined to interpret the constitution so as to limit them as much as possible; and, during his presidency, the advice of the senate, previous to the negotiation of a treaty, was never requested.[2]

The practice of Adams has been followed since with but few exceptions. The first of these is that of Jackson, who consulted the senate previous to the negotiation of a treaty with the Choctaws. In the message asking the senate for its advice he said: "I am fully aware that in thus resorting to the earlier practice of the Senate in the discharge of this portion of my duties, I am departing from a long and for many years an unbroken usage in similar cases. But being satisfied that this resort is consistent with the provision of the Constitution; that it is strongly recommended in this instance by considerations of expediency; and that the reasons which have led to the observance of a different practice, though very cogent in negotiations with foreign nations, do not apply with equal force to those made with the Indian tribes, I

[1] Exec. Jour., I, 27, 28.

[2] Soon after entering office Adams asked Wolcott if certain instructions to a foreign minister should be laid before the senate for their advice and consent before being sent to Europe, and Wolcott replied that he did not think it wise to consult the senate on treaties, previous to their negotiation, as it did not possess sufficient information to enable it to act wisely, and because such a course would render secrecy impossible. (Gibbs, Administration of Washington and Adams., I, 516, 517.)

flatter myself that it will not meet with the disapprobation of the Senate."[1]

The report of the committee of the senate to whom the message and treaty was referred contained only vague recommendations; and even these were not adopted by the senate, the committee, in accordance with its request, being discharged,[2] and no further action being taken on the subject, the senate thus showing itself less eager to extend its influence than the president seemed to expect. Yet Madison, writing about this time, gives the claim of a right to be consulted, previous to the negotiation of a treaty, as among the innovating doctrines of the senate,[3] and Benton says that the view was held by many senators.[4]

The previous consultation of the senate by Polk in negotiating the treaty with Great Britain for the settlement of the Oregon controversy, was undoubtedly due to a desire to throw the responsibility for the treaty on the senate. He declared in his message, however, that he approved of the practice on momentous questions, because it would secure harmony in the actions of the executive department; and, in this case, was especially advisable since peace or war might depend on the decision of the question.[5]

The same question was also the occasion of the next consultation of the senate previous to the negotiation of a treaty. The treaty of 1846 was not decisive on certain points concerning the boundary between Oregon and the English possessions; and, after several unsuccessful attempts at settlement, the president submitted the question to the senate, and asked if they would agree to a treaty of arbitration with certain specific fea-

[1] Exec. Jour., IV, 98.
[2] *Ibid.*, 112, 119.
[3] Works, IV, 370.
[4] Thirty Years' View, II, 675.
[5] *Ibid.*, pp. 673, 675.

tures.[1] The senate adjourning before it had taken action on the subject, and Lincoln coming to the presidency, the senate sent to him a copy of the message of his predecessor, and Lincoln, in acknowledging this, says: "I find no reason to disapprove of the course of my predecessor in this important matter, but, on the contrary, I not only shall receive the advice of the Senate thereon cheerfully, but I respectfully ask the Senate for their advice."[2] This the senate accordingly gave.[3]

Lincoln again consulted the senate in December, 1861, regarding a convention with Mexico, submitting to that body for its advice a copy of a draft for a convention proposed to the government of Mexico by Mr. Corwin, the minister of the United States.[4] Later he communicated a letter of the minister, asking for instructions, and requested the advice of the senate on the pending treaty.[5] The senate adopted a resolution expressing its disapproval of the treaty, and making general suggestions regarding another, while stating that the lack of information made it impossible to go into details.[6] President Johnson in 1869 submitted a protocol with Great Britain to the senate for its advice as to the expediency of concluding a convention based thereon,[7] and President Grant asked the advice of the senate regarding the indemnities in the Alabama affair.

When, as has happened on a few occasions, the president has asked for an appropriation of money for the

[1] Exec. Jour., XI, 279, 282.

[2] *Ibid.*, pp. 307, 308.

[3] *Ibid.*, p. 314.

[4] *Ibid.*, XII, p. 24.

[5] *Ibid.*, p. 102.

[6] The communication of the opinion of the senate by the president to Mr. Corwin failed to reach him, and the proposed treaty was, therefore, negotiated. When received, Lincoln submitted it with an explanation of the circumstances to the senate, by which it was tabled. (Exec. Jour., XII, pp. 370, 401.)

[7] Exec. Jour., XVI, pp. 441, 477.

purposes of the negotiation of a treaty, the senate has thus had an opportunity, incidentally, to say whether it wished such a treaty negotiated.[1] Similarly the senate in confirming a minister for the purpose of negotiating a treaty gives its consent to that negotiation. In most cases, however, even this opportunity for the expression of an opinion, prior to the negotiation of a treaty, is not given to the senate; for most of our treaties have been negotiated by the ministers resident in the country with which the treaty was to be made, or by secret agents of the president who were private citizens or officers of the government commissioned for that purpose. In 1888 the number of persons who had been so appointed by the president was four hundred thirty-eight while but thirty-two had been appointed with the advice of the senate; and, between 1827 and 1880, none were so appointed, although many of the appointments during this time were made when the senate was in session.[2]

Objections have, on several occasions, been made to the employment of private agents for the negotiation of treaties, and considerable discussion has taken place; but on one occasion only has the senate adopted a resolution expressive of its disapproval of such a course. This was in 1831,[3] and, when three years later a similar resolution was introduced, it was at once tabled;[4] while in 1838, when Van Buren was about to commission our chargé d'affaires to Peru to stop on his way at Ecuador to negotiate a treaty, and communicated this fact to the senate in order to give it an opportunity, if it wished,

[1] Such an appropriation was made in 1803 (Annals of Congr., 2d Sess., 7th Congr., pp. 91-96, 102, 103, 106-255), and in 1806 (Exec. Jour., II, 36-43), and was asked for in 1846 (Exec. Jour., VII, p. 133).

[2] Report of Committee on Foreign Affairs, 1st Sess., 50th Congr., Sen. Misc. Docs., vol. 2, No. 109, pp. 103, 104.

[3] Congr. Debates, vol. VII, 2d Sess., 21st Congr., p. 310, yeas 25, nays 18.

[4] Exec. Jour., IV, 445.

for the expression of an opinion on the exercise of such a power by the executive,[1] no action was taken beyond the reference of the message to a committee; and a treaty, presumably negotiated in the manner suggested, was afterward adopted.

A resolution of Mr. Chandler of July 20, 1888,[2] denying the right of the president to appoint private citizens as special agents, called forth the report which showed how frequently this had been done.

Though the senate, through its power of confirmation, does not often have an opportunity to say whether a specified treaty shall be negotiated, and only in a few instances has been requested to give its advice previous to or during a negotiation, it nevertheless frequently, especially of late years, exercises a considerable influence in the formation of treaties. Ordinarily it may obtain any information regarding negotiations, during their progress, by the adoption of a resolution calling for such information,[3] which the president, knowing that he must finally obtain the consent of the senate to whatever is done, will be inclined to communicate, if it can be done without prejudice to existing negotiations. Then the senate has, occasionally, though it has been objected to by some as unconstitutional, adopted resolutions requesting the president to pursue a certain policy. These, however, are of rare occurrence, and had the influence of the senate depended upon them alone, it would have been slight; but the president, in view of the fact that all his negotiations must eventually be passed upon by the senate, finds it necessary to defer to their wishes to a certain extent; consequently, there is a great deal of informal communication between the president or secretary of foreign affairs and senators or com-

[1] Exec. Jour., V, p. 119.

[2] Congr. Record, 1st Sess., 50th Congr., pp. 6568.

[3] *Ibid.*, 1st Sess., 49th Congr., pp. 2216-2220, for list of such calls.

mittees of the senate, the influence of the chairman of the committee on foreign affairs being the greatest.

The power of the senate in this regard seems to have increased considerably of late. The *Nation* in 1872 says: "The conduct of the Senate during the past ten years on questions of foreign policy has been such that it will hereafter be very difficult, if not increasingly difficult, for the President to enter on any negotiation with any foreign power on his own motion, or from his own sense of fitness or expediency. The relations between him and the Senate have, as every-body knows, of late undergone serious and important, though not always perceptible modifications."[1] And Mr. Morgan, when the tendency of the senate to control all diplomatic affairs was shown in its action on the fisheries treaty, said: "The Senate has become of late years extremely aggressive in its endeavor to control by resolutions, and through the action of the committees, the whole diplomatic relations."[2]

When a treaty has been negotiated, the president has assumed the right to reject it without submission to the senate, if he deemed it unwise;[3] and, in one case, that of the extradition treaty with the Netherlands of May 29, 1856, the president, after submitting it to the senate, requested its return, and the senate complied with the request. The treaty was re-submitted a few months later and ratified with amendments. The president in laying a treaty before the senate has also suggested amendments;[4] and, in one case, that of the treaty of 1863 with Peru, the treaty was formally amended before submission to the senate.[5]

[1] *Nation*, May 30, 1872, p. 348.

[2] Congr. Record, 1st Sess., 50th Congr., p. 8672.

[3] Such was Jefferson's course of procedure in regard to the treaty of December 31, 1806, with Great Britain, and such that of Polk in regard to the treaty with Mexico of March 15, 1854.

[4] Exec. Jour., VIII, 290, IX, 266, XI, 256.

[5] *Ibid.*, XIII, 122.

When a treaty has been agreed to by the senate, on condition that ratifications should be made within a certain time, and this has not been done, it has been customary to submit the treaty to the senate for a second ratification.[1]

With one exception a law or resolution of congress has been considered necessary for the abrogation of treaties, it being held that, since treaties are by the constitution declared to be "the supreme law of the land," they could be abrogated by no power less than that which abrogates existing laws, which is the congress.[2]

The first instance of the abrogation of a treaty on our part was that of the French treaty in 1798. The joint resolution declaring the treaty to be void was introduced in the senate, and no notice appears in the recorded proceedings of any other possible mode of action being suggested.

When later the termination of the convention with Great Britain regarding the joint occupancy of Oregon was desired, the president recommended its repeal by law, and congress complied with the recommendation. There were some, at that time, who held that the same power should be required for the abrogation of a treaty as for its conclusion, and, in the second session of the Thirty-third Congress, the senate in secret session unanimously adopted a resolution authorizing the president, at his discretion, to give notice to Denmark of the termination of the treaty with that power;[3] it being held that a law of congress was not necessary as the treaty con-

[1] J. Q. Adams, Works, V, 285; Exec. Jour., IV, 7, 9, 147, 151; V, 244, 275; VIII, 385.

[2] This was the view taken by Story (Commentaries, sec. 1838), and upheld by Judge Iredell in a judicial decision. (Ware vs. Hylton *et al.*; 1 Curtis, 205.)

[3] Exec. Jour., IX, 431.

tained provision for its termination.[1] The notice, in accordance with the senate resolution, was given and, at the next session, the senate refused to consider a resolution, introduced by Mr. Sumner in open session, directing the committee of foreign affairs to consider if an act of congress was not necessary for the abrogation of a treaty.[2] The resolution of Mr. Sumner had been caused by a proposal made in executive session and favorably reported by a committee, for the abrogation by resolution of the senate of certain articles of a treaty with Great Britain;[3] and, though the resolution was never voted upon, it was feared at the time that there was an intention of reviving it.

The action in the case of the Denmark treaty has not been made a precedent, and, though there are still some who hold that a treaty may be abrogated by the president and senate, the practice has conformed to the earlier mode, the joint resolution often being introduced in the senate, as in the abrogation in 1883 of the fisheries article of the treaty with Great Britian.[4]

That a law of congress in contradiction of treaty stipulations repealed them has always been held.[5]

[1] The treaty with Great Britain regarding the joint occupancy of Oregon contained provision for its termination, but it was not held, on that account, that a law was unnecessary for its abrogation; nor was this held in regard to the treaty of 1854 with Great Britain which was abrogated by law in 1865.

[2] Sumner, Works, IV, 99.

[3] Exec. Jour., IX, 330, 334.

[4] Congr. Record, 2d Sess., 47th Congr., p. 3056.

[5] This is shown by the law of 1816 for regulating the tonnage, from which it is seen that it was considered necessary, if the provisions of treaties were not to be abrogated by the law, to state this to be the case (Statutes at Large, vol. III, p. 314, 1st Sess., 14th Congr., chap. 107, sec. 6). A law of 1817 (*Ibid.*, vol. III, p. 344, 2d Sess., 14th Congr., chap. 3, sec. 1), and one of 1862 (*Ibid.*, vol. XII, p. 558, 2d Sess., 37th Congr., chap. 163, sec. 15) shows the same; and this view has been upheld by judicial decisions. (Taylor vs. Morton, C. C. R., 2 Curtis, 454; and Cherokee Tobacco Case, 11 Wall, 621. "A law of Congress repugnant to a treaty to that extent abrogates it.")

Although in the clauses of the constitution referring to treaties, nothing is said of any share of the house in them, such part has been claimed by the house. That such a claim should have been made is due to the fact that many treaties contain stipulations regarding subjects, which, by the constitution, are specifically confided to congress, or may be inferred to be granted to that body.

Especially in Indian treaties has the house claimed, and exercised, a considerable influence, since nearly all such treaties involve the payment of money or the disposal of the public lands, in the latter of which the house considers that it has an equal right of deciding, and in the former a preponderating.

Washington recognized this claim of the house by consulting and receiving instructions from it before proceeding with negotiations.[1] The usual practice was for congress to make appropriations for Indian treaties prior to their negotiation. Sometimes the appropriations were made in general terms, sometimes specific sums were appropriated for negotiations with specified tribes, and sometimes laws were passed authorizing the president to enter into negotiations for treaties with certain tribes, no special appropriation being made for the purpose.[2] Occasionally, however, treaties involving the payment of money were made without a previous appropriation, congress afterwards making it.

In 1838 a resolution was submitted in the senate forbidding the president to have negotiated, without a previous appropriation by congress, any treaty with the Indians for the purchase or exchange of land;[3] and bills and joint resolutions, denying the right of the senate and the executive, by treaty with the Indians, to dispose

[1] Annals of Congress, 1st Sess., 1st Congr., pp. 60, 710, 711.

[2] See Statutes at Large, under Indian treaties. Also Congr. Globe, 1st Sess., 40th Congr., p. 374, and 1st Sess., 41st Congr., p. 167.

[3] Exec. Jour., V, p. 138.

of the public domain, except by direct conveyance to the United States, were repeatedly introduced in the house, but pigeon-holed in the senate.[1]

An increase in the practice of negotiating Indian treaties without any previous law was acquiesced in by the house for some years, and the Indian policy practically left to the senate;[2] but in 1867 a law was passed, on a bill making appropriations for deficiencies in the contingent expenses of the senate, which provided that: "All laws allowing the President, the Secretary of the Interior, or the Commissioner of Indian affairs to enter into treaties with any Indian tribes are hereby repealed, and no expenses shall hereafter be incurred in negotiating a treaty with any Indian tribe until an appropriation authorizing such an expense shall be first made by law."[3] The exigencies of an Indian war made it necessary to repeal this law soon after,[4] but in 1871 it was finally agreed that no treaty should thereafter be made with an Indian tribe.[5]

The infringement of treaties regulating commerce, acquiring or ceding territory, or providing for the payment of money, upon the powers granted to congress, has led the house to claim a discretionary power in carrying into effect treaties containing regulations on any of these subjects; and it has been able to enforce its claim through the necessity for legislative action to carry such treaties into effect. This claim was first made in connection with the Jay treaty, which excited much partisan feeling, and was ratified by the bare two-thirds vote required. The treaty provided for the pay-

[1] Congr. Globe, 1st Sess., 41st Congr., p. 57, statement of Mr. Julian.

[2] *Ibid.*, pp. 147, 166; and 1st Sess., 40th Congr., p. 374, statement of Mr. Sherman.

[3] Statutes at Large, vol. XV, p. 9, 1st Sess., 40th Congr., chap. 13, sec. 6.

[4] *Ibid.*, p. 18, chap. 34.

[5] *Ibid.*, vol. XVI, p. 566, 3d Sess., 41st Congr., chap. 120.

ment of a small sum of money, and its promulgation before its submission to the house naturally irritated those who claimed for the house a discretionary power in carrying such treaties into effect. The opposition was begun by the introduction of a resolution calling upon the president for papers relating to the treaty, with the avowed object of discussing the constitutional question. This called forth a debate of nearly a month, in the course of which the different views were set forth.[1] The resolution was finally adopted by a large majority.[2] Washington, with the approval of his cabinet, refused to comply with the request, stating among his reasons for doing so that the house had no right to deliberate on a treaty, it having become obligatory when ratified by the president and senate.[3] The appropriation was finally voted by the house, a resolution being previously adopted, which, while disclaiming for the house any agency in making treaties, declared that, "when a treaty stipulates regulations on any of the subjects submitted by the Constitution to the power of Congress, it must depend for its execution, as to such stipulations, on a law or laws to be passed by Congress."[4]

Jefferson, the leader of the Republicans, when he became president, recognized the claims of the house. Speaking of the instruments for the transfer of Louisiana he said: "When these shall have received the constitutional sanction of the Senate, they will, without delay, be communicated to the House of Representatives for the exercise of their functions, as to those conditions which are within the powers vested by the Constitution in Congress."[5] He also on one occasion requested congress to make a secret appropriation for the negotiation

[1] Annals of Congress, 1st Sess., 4th Congr., pp. 426 ff.

[2] *Ibid.*, 1st Sess., 4th Congr., p. 759, yeas 62, nays 37.

[3] *Ibid.*, 1st Sess., 4th Congr., pp. 760, 761.

[4] *Ibid.*, 1st Sess., 4th Congr., pp. 771, 782, 783.

[5] *Ibid.*, 1st Sess., 8th Congr., p. 12.

of a treaty;[1] and, at another time, when, without his formal request,[2] such an appropriation had been made by congress,[3] he stated that he considered it as conveying the sanction of congress to the acquisition proposed.[4]

In 1816 the position of both houses was clearly set forth in connection with the convention of 1815 with Great Britain, which was in contradiction to certain of our revenue laws. The senate held that these laws were repealed by the treaty and that no act of congress was necessary; but the house thought otherwise and the senate finally yielded and consented to the passage of an act repealing the laws, it being agreed that it should not be taken as a precedent.[5] The position of the senate has been upheld by an attorney general,[6] but the supreme court takes the opposite view.[7]

The right to acquire or cede territory by means of the treaty-making power has also been questioned. Jefferson thought that this power did not reside in any part of the government. The purchase made by him and that of 1819,[8] however, were acquiesced in and their legality confirmed by a decision of the supreme court in favor of the power of the government to "acquire new territory either by conquest or by treaty;"[9] but the question again came up for discussion when the annexation of Texas was under consideration.

[1] Exec. Jour., II, 36-43.

[2] 1st Sess., 33d Congr., p. 1563, statement of Mr. Benton.

[3] Annals of Congr., 2d Sess., 7th Congr., pp. 90, 104.

[4] *Ibid.*, 1st Sess., 8th Congr., p. 12.

[5] *Ibid.*, 1st Sess., 14th Congr., pp. 46 ff.

[6] 13 Op., 355.

[7] Foster v. Neilson, 2 Peters, 314.

[8] The treaty was adopted unanimously, but at the next session Mr. Clay introduced a resolution, which excited much debate, declaring that no treaty for alienating the territory of the United States was valid without the consent of congress. It was held then that the consent might be given after the ratification. (Clay, Works, V, 206.)

[9] Am. Insurance Co. *et al.*, v Canter, 1 Peters, 542.

Some held that the settlement of boundary disputes, only, belonged to the treaty making power,[1] and that for the acquisition or cession of territory the consent of congress was necessary. This view was based on the clause of the constitution which gives to congress the right to dispose of territories or other property of the United States and that which gives congress power to admit new states.[2] There were a greater number who, while acknowledging that foreign territory might be acquired by treaty, denied the right to incorporate another nation by treaty.[3] The annexation of Texas by treaty was also objected to because it would be the adoption of the war with Mexico, and it was held that the president and the senate had no right to make war either by declaration or adoption.[4]

So many reasons, other than the constitutional ones, operated to secure the rejection of the treaty that it is impossible to infer from it that there was a majority in the senate who held the acquisition of this territory, by treaty, to be unconstitutional; just as it is impossible to infer from the adoption of the joint resolution introduced in the house[5] for the acquisition of Texas, that a majority of both houses considered that the constitutional mode of acquiring foreign territory.

The request of President Polk, prior to the negotiation of the treaty with Mexico, for an appropriation to be used, if necessary, in the negotiation, does not seem to have been regarded by him as a request for a previous

[1] Congr. Globe, 1st Sess., 28th Congr., p. 656, and p. 658, note.

[2] *Ibid.*, 1st Sess., 28th Congr., p. 656, note; 2d Sess., 28th Congr., p. 280.

[3] *Ibid.*, 1st Sess., 28th Congr., App., pp. 539, 682, 722.

[4] *Ibid.*, 1st Sess., 28th Congr., App., p. 474. For arguments for and against, see pp. 539, 558, 559, 685, 695.

[5] The senate committee on foreign relations reported against the adoption of the house resolution on the ground that it was unconstitutional, holding that foreign territory could be acquired only by treaty. (2d Sess., 28th Congr., Sen. Misc. Docs., vol. III, No. 79.)

legislative sanction.[1] The senate, however, took the opportunity to advise the president to take all proper measures to secure peace, and signified its willingness to make the appropriation required.[2]

When the Gadsden treaty, which appropriated a large sum for the purchase of foreign territory, was under consideration, the acquisition of foreign territory without authorization from congress was again declared to be a breach of the privileges of the house,[3] the assertion, however, being warmly contested.[4] Nearly all seem to have conceded the right to grant or withhold the appropriation, though the call for papers was not made, it being resisted by the president's party.

The next discussion on the subject was over the appropriation for the treaty of 1867 with Russia for the purchase of Alaska. The fourth article of the treaty provided: "But the cession, with the right of immediate possession, is nevertheless to be deemed complete and absolute on the exchange of the ratifications;"[5] and the actual delivery of the territory had taken place before the appropriation for executing the treaty was made,[6] and the president in his message assumed that the house must pass the appropriation.[7]

In the house this invasion of its rights, as it was called, was discussed quite as much as the expediency of the treaty An amendment to the bill making the

[1] Exec. Jour., VII, 133.

[2] *Ibid.*, VII, 137, 139.

[3] Congr. Globe, 1st Sess., 33d Congr , vol. 28, part ii, pp. 15, 19.

[4] *Ibid.*, 1st Sess., 33d Congr., vol. 28, part ii, pp. 1561, 1563.

[5] *Ibid.*, 2d Sess., 40th Congr., p. 1871.

[6] *Ibid.*, 2d Sess., 40th Congr., p. 1871.

[7] "It will hardly be necessary to call the attention of Congress to the subject of providing for the payment to Russia of the sum stipulated in the treaty for the cession of Alaska. Possession having been formally delivered to our commissioner, the territory remains for the present in care of a military force." (Annual Messages ed. by Poore, 1867, p. 23.)

appropriation, providing that thereafter no purchase of foreign territory should be concluded until after provision had been made by law for payment, and denying that the president and senate had, by the constitution, a right to complete the purchase of foreign territory before the necessary appropriation had been made by an act of congress, was lost in the house by two votes only;[1] and it was agreed, by a vote of 98 to 49, to prefix to the bill making the appropriation a preamble stating that, inasmuch as the payment of money, the accepting of the cession of territory, and the stipulation that the Russians should have all the rights and privileges of American citizens, were subjects submitted to the powers of congress, to which, therefore, the consent of congress was necessary to give to them full force and validity, congress had taken into consideration the said treaty and agreed to its stipulations.[2] This was stricken out in the senate without debate;[3] and the subject going to a conference committee a preamble was substituted which, while acknowledging that the subjects referred to were within the power of congress, and that they could not be carried into full force and effect without the consent of both houses of congress, struck out that portion of the preamble, adopted by the house, which stated that congress had taken the treaty into consideration, and also the first section of the bill which declared the assent of congress to the treaty.[4] In the senate this report was accepted without debate and in the house by a vote of 91 to 48. This was advocated both because of the necessity of passing the appropriation, it being thought that the house had sufficiently defined its posi-

[1] Congr. Globe, 2d Sess., 40th Congr., p. 4055, yeas 78, nays 80, 40 not voting.

[2] *Ibid.*, 2d Sess., 40th Congr., p. 4055.

[3] *Ibid.*, p. 4159.

[4] *Ibid.*, p. 4404.

tion,[1] and because it was, in effect, the same as the resolution first adopted.[2]

As has been seen, the senate in 1816 held that no act of congress was necessary to render valid commercial regulations contained in a treaty. In 1832, when a convention with France which contained an article regulating the duties on French wine was under consideration,[3] a resolution, introduced in the senate by Mr. Clay, stating that the senate entertained objections to that article which would have been decisive against its provisions if the article had stood alone, and that they did not think that it should be taken as a precedent in the future exercise of the treaty making power, was tabled.[4]

When in 1844 the commercial treaty with the Germanic Zollverein was submitted to the senate, it changed its position and took ground as extreme as any ever urged in the other house.[5] Tyler, in submitting the treaty, said: "Inasmuch as the provisions of the treaty come to some extent in conflict with existing laws, it is my intention, should it receive your approval and ratification, to communicate a copy of it to the House of Representatives, in order that the House may take such action upon it as it may deem necessary to give efficiency to its provisions."[6]

The senate committee of foreign affairs, to whom the treaty was referred, reported that they believed the control of trade, and the function of taxing, were indisputably given to congress, and that they were not prepared

[1] Congr. Globe, 2d Sess., 40th Congr., p. 4393, urged by Mr. Loughbridge.

[2] *Ibid.*, p. 4394, urged by Mr. Banks.

[3] Statutes at Large, vol. VIII, p. 432, Art. VII.

[4] Exec. Jour., IV, 209.

[5] This treaty changed duties laid by law, and put it beyond the power of congress to exceed the stipulated maximum of duties on imports, for at least three years.

[6] Exec. Jour., VI, 263.

to sanction so large an innovation as the adoption of the present treaty would be, "upon ancient and uniform practice in respect of the *Department of Government* by which duties on imports should be imposed."[1] The next day after the report was made, the convention was laid upon the table by a vote of 26 to 18, which, it would seem, should indicate the views of the members on the constitutional question, as that was the only objection made to it; but Calhoun says that it was defeated from strictly party motives,[2] and this statement is supported by the fact that the eighteen who voted against tabling the convention were Democrats, being the direct descendants of the strict construction Republicans, who, in 1795, had wished to restrict so closely the power of the president and senate in making treaties.

The president not regarding this action of the senate as final, again submitted the question to it,[3] when the committee re-affirmed their former report, stating that the object of the committee in its former action "was to reach the end of the refusal to ratify the convention in the mode most conformable to the comity due to the parties to it."[4] The committee, while declaring that the power of the president and senate to interfere in the regulation of imports was not contested, or the possible occurrence of an occasion where it might be advisable, held that in the present case it was not so.

Since then the senate has frequently exercised this power, though not without objection being made. In 1885 the house committee on the judiciary made an elaborate report on the powers of the executive in making treaties affecting the tariff, which was accompanied by a resolution declaring: "That the President, by and with

[1] Exec. Jour., VI, p. 333.

[2] Winsor, Narrative and Critical History, vol. VII, p. 512, citing Lawrence, Wheaton's International Law, ed. 1863, p. liv.

[3] Exec. Jour., VI, 357.

[4] *Ibid.*, 407.

the advice and consent of the Senate, cannot negotiate treaties with foreign governments, by which the duties levied by Congress can be changed or abrogated; and such treaties to be operative as laws, must have the sanction of Congress."[1] The disapproval of the regulation of duties by the treaty-making power was also shown by proposals for an amendment to the constitution requiring the prior consent of congress to reciprocity treaties; and one for the election of senators by the people, because the senate was arrogating to itself the power of levying taxes by treaties.

There are a few instances in which treaties regulating the revenue have recognized the rights of the house by requiring that the treaty should not go into effect until congress had passed the laws necessary to put it in operation. Such a provision was contained in the reciprocity treaty of 1854 with Great Britain,[2] in the reciprocity treaty of 1875 with Hawaii,[3] and in that of 1883 with Mexico.[4] In the latter case the necessary legislation was never passed by the congress of the United States.

The decision of the circuit court of the United States is in favor of the position taken by the house. It is held that, in the execution of a treaty which stipulates for the payment of money, the representatives "exercise their own judgment in granting or withholding the money. They act upon their own responsibility, and not upon the responsibility of the treaty-making power. It cannot bind or control the legislative action in this respect, and every foreign government may be presumed to know that, so far as the treaty stipulates to pay money, the legislative sanction is required."[5]

[1] 2d Sess., 48th Congr., House Res., No. 2680.

[2] Statutes at Large, vol. X, p. 1092, Art. V.

[3] Treaties and Conventions, 1776–1887, p. 548, Art. V.

[4] *Ibid.*, p. 718, Art. VIII.

[5] Turner vs. Am. Baptist Church, 5 McLean's C. C. R., 347.

The United States, however, did not recognize this in 1834, in the case of France, when it was maintained that a failure to execute a treaty, duly made and ratified by the proper authorities, was a sufficient cause for war. Such is also the view taken by high authorities on international law. Pomeroy says that the neglect or refusal of congress to carry out the provisions of a treaty, would be a sufficient cause for war;[1] and Wheaton that, as a matter of international law, there is no doubt that the nation is bound.[2]

[1] Constitutional Law, p. 450, sec. 676.

[2] International Law, p. 339, sec. 266, note. Halleck (International Law, vol. I, p. 234) holds the same; and much the same view is taken by Attorney General Cushing, who says: "Such action may be regarded as a political duty under ordinary circumstances, and in no case has such legislation been heretofore refused." (6 Op., Cushing, 1854.)

## CHAPTER V.

### THE SENATE AS A JUDICIAL BODY.

THE judicial functions of the senate have rarely been exercised, there having been but seven trials in the period of over a hundred years since the organization of the government under the present constitution.[1]

The first trial was that of Senator Blount in 1798. Documents containing evidence of his guilt were transmitted by the president to both houses at the same time, and the senate was considering his conduct when the resolution for impeachment was received from the house. This was near the end of the session, and a couple of months of the next session had passed by before the articles of impeachment were received; and the trial did not take place until the following session.

The articles of impeachment exhibited by the house charged Blount with setting on foot, on the western frontiers, an expedition to conquer the territories of Spain and transfer them to Great Britain; with exciting the Indians to attack the Spanish; with corruption of the Indian interpreter, and attempts to alienate the confidence of the Indians from our agent; and with endeavoring to excite the Indians against the United States, over the settlement of certain boundary questions. Blount not appearing at the trial, he was allowed to be heard by counsel, who pleaded a lack of jurisdiction on the part of the senate. They maintained:

"I. That only civil officers of the United States are impeachable; and that the offences for which an Im-

[1] These were of Senator Blount in 1798, Judge Pickering in 1803, Judge Chase in 1804 and 1805, Judge Peck in 1830, Judge Humphries in 1862, President Johnson in 1868, and Secretary Belknap in 1876.

peachment lies, must be committed in the execution of a public office.

"II. That a Senator is not a civil officer, impeachable within the meaning of the Constitution; and that, in the present instance, no crime or misdemeanor is charged to have been committed by William Blount in the character of a Senator."[1]

The right of the senate to try a person impeached, after his expulsion from office, was also questioned.

The question of jurisdiction was argued for and against by the managers and counsel for four days, and then considered by the senate in secret session for four days more, when it was decided, fourteen to eleven, that William Blount was not a civil officer within the meaning of the constitution of the United States, and therefore was not liable to be impeached by the house of representatives.[2]

This far reaching decision, which removed all senators and representatives from the fear of impeachment, and which, according to Rawle, was undoubtedly contrary to the intention of the constitution, was very severely criticised at the time; and the senate later put on record its belief that senators and representatives are civil officers, by holding that the oath prescribed for "civil officers," by the act of 1862, must be taken by senators.

The next person to be impeached was John Pickering, a judge of the federal district court of New Hampshire. He was charged with decisions contrary to law and with drunkenness and profanity on the bench.[3] Pickering failing to appear when summoned, either in person or by counsel, a letter from his son was read, stating that his father was insane, and asking for time in which to collect proofs of it. Enclosed was also a letter of Mr. Harper asking that he might be allowed to appear

[1] Annals of Congress, 1st Sess., 5th Congr., p. 2263.

[2] *Ibid.*, p. 2318.

[3] See Articles of Impeachment.

on behalf of the petitioner, since it was impossible for any one to appear as attorney or agent of the judge, as he was insane.[1]

The managers on the part of the house objected to this;[2] but the senate, after debate, decided that they would "hear evidence and counsel respecting the insanity of John Pickering."[3] As the managers did not feel themselves under any obligation to discuss a preliminary question thus raised by a third person, unauthorized by the person accused, they withdrew to take the opinion of the house as to their future action. The senate refusing to adjourn until they should hear further from them, Mr. Harper was immediately heard in support of the plea of insanity. The next day the senate notified the managers that it was ready to hear evidence in support of the articles of impeachment. Accordingly, on March eighth, the trial was continued. The argument of the managers and the taking of testimony occupied two days; when, the senate having refused to postpone the decision to give time for further testimony to be produced, the judge was declared guilty by a strict party vote, all the Federalists voting not guilty, and removed from office; but the further disqualification to hold office was not added.[4]

Scarcely was judgment pronounced in the case of Pickering when the impeachment of Samuel Chase, associate justice of the supreme court, was received. At that time a custom prevailed to a certain extent, both here and in England, of delivering a political speech in the charge to the grand jury. Chase was a strong Federalist and the delivery by him of such a speech, in which he criticised severely certain acts of the Republicans, excited much indignation and led to his impeach-

[1] Annals of Congress, 1st Sess., 8th Congr., p. 330.
[2] *Ibid.*, p. 331.
[3] *Ibid.*, p. 333.
[4] *Ibid.*, pp. 362-368.

ment. The eighth article of impeachment was based on this speach, which it declared was delivered with intent to excite the grand jury and people against the governments of the United States and Maryland. The charges made in the other seven articles were brought to light by the investigation of the house committee in his career as judge, belonging to a period of time five years earlier, and charged him with arbitrary, oppressive, and unjust conduct in the trial of certain cases.

Chase, while acknowledging that he had in most cases done as charged by the articles of impeachment, denied the motives imputed to him for so doing, and declared that, in each case, he believed himself to be acting in strict accordance with justice and right, and that if he were wrong it was an error of judgment, and not a crime, that he had committed. He called attention to the precedents for the action charged in the eighth article, and pointed out that, as he had violated no law, he could not be punished.[1]

The trial lasted nearly a month, when the vote was taken and the judge acquitted, there being but two articles on which a majority pronounced him guilty, and this although there was a strong Republican majority in the senate.

The next person tried was James Peck, a judge of the federal district court of Missouri. He was charged by the house with having arbitrarily, unjustly, and oppressively, under color and pretence of law, punished for contempt of court a certain attorney who had published in a newspaper a criticism of a decision of Judge Peck on a land case.[2] The action referred to had been taken in 1826, but it was not until 1830 that the impeachment was decided upon, though attempts to procure his impeachment had been made before.

[1] Annals of Congress, 2d Sess., 8th Congr., 102 ff.

[2] See Articles of Impeachment, Congr. Debates, 1st Sess., 21st Congr., pp. 411, 412.

The judge in his defence asserted that the paper referred to was a contempt of court, because it misrepresented the opinion of the court, which it professed to censure, and tended to excite the public mind against it; and, moreover, that he was justified in believing that this misrepresentation was willfully, wantonly, and maliciously made. He further maintained that if he were wrong in this, it was an error of judgment, and not a misdemeanor willfully and knowingly done in violation of the law, or with the intention imputed in the articles of impeachment.[1]

The trial began in the first session of the Twenty-first Congress, when the answer of the respondent was filed. It was then postponed until the next session, in which it continued uninterruptedly from December 20th to January 31st, when Peck was declared not guilty.[2]

The next trial was that of West H. Humphries, judge of the federal district court of Tennessee, who, though actively engaged in the war of the rebellion, had not resigned his position as United States judge. Impeachment, therefore, became necessary to render the office vacant. He was accordingly impeached, and tried in due form, though naturally he neither appeared in person nor by attorney at the trial. The seven articles of impeachment were based on a secession speech delivered at Nashville in 1860, and on his acceptance of the office of confederate judge, and he was convicted by the unanimous vote of the senate.

The next trial, that of President Johnson, is the most important one, both because it was the trial of the chief officer of the United States, and because of the strong partisan feeling connected with it, which made this trial the most severe test of the justice and impartiality of the senate as a judicial body which it has ever undergone.

[1] Sen. Jour., 2d Sess., 21st Congr., App., pp. 251–321.

[2] Twenty-two voting not guilty, and twenty-one guilty.

The conflict between President Johnson and congress had caused several proposals of impeachment to be made. In November, 1867, the judiciary committee, after a long investigation, reported in favor of an impeachment,[1] but the resolution was rejected by the house ;[2] and it was not until the removal of Secretary Stanton, contrary to the tenure of office act as held by both houses, and the appointment of Thomas as secretary *ad interim*, that the impeachment of the president was resolved upon. Stanton had refused to vacate his office, and at once communicated to the house of representatives notice of his attempted removal. The same day a resolution for the impeachment of the president was submitted, and, after being debated for three days, was adopted.[3]

The promptitude with which this impeachment was carried through, was something new. The resolution of impeachment was communicated to the senate the 25th of February, and on March 4th the articles of impeachment were presented. These were eleven in number. The first three charged the president with violation of the tenure of office act in the removal of Stanton and appointment of Thomas. The next three charged him with conspiracy with Thomas, and others unknown, for the violation of the tenure of office act, and the seizure by force of the property of the United States in the department of war. The eighth article related to the alleged attempts, by means of the appointment of Thomas, to control the disbursements of the money in the military service. The ninth article charged the president with attempting to induce General Emory to violate the act regulating the military service ; while articles ten and eleven charged him with designing and intending to set

[1] Congr. Globe, 1st Sess., 40th Congr., pp. 791, 792.
[2] *Ibid.*, 2d Sess., 40th Congr., pp. 67, 68.
[3] *Ibid.*, 2d Sess., 40th Congr., pp. 1329, 1400.

aside the lawful authority of congress, by exciting the people against it, by scandalous and inflammatory speeches, and by declaring that the Thirty-ninth Congress was no congress. The eleventh article also charged him with "unlawfully devising and contriving" means to prevent the execution of the tenure of office act, the act for the regulation of the army, and the reconstruction acts.

The president in reply to the first three articles denied that Stanton's case came under the provisions of the tenure of office act, inasmuch as he was appointed by President Lincoln, and had not been reappointed; he therefore held that there was a vacancy existing when Thomas was appointed. He further denied that the removal of Stanton was made with intent to violate the tenure of office act, and also that there was a conspiracy with Thomas, and he declared that he only said to Emory in conversation what he had also said in messages to congress. In answer to articles ten and eleven he claimed the right of freedom of speech, and he denied that he had ever said that the Thirty-ninth Congress was not a congress, or had attempted to evade the execution of the laws. He also called attention to the fact that the charges made in these last articles did not relate to any official wrong doing or misconduct.

As the total number of senators was fifty-four, and twelve of these were Democrats, who would be sure to vote not guilty, there could be no conviction should the proof offered fail to convince seven of the Republican senators, and this was what happened. Several Republican senators held that, inasmuch as at the time of the passage of the tenure of office act, it was admitted that it did not apply to the cabinet officers of Mr. Lincoln, they could not therefore vote guilty on the Stanton articles. On the Emory and conspiracy articles the proof was weak, and the tenth article was based on unofficial utterances. Before the end of the trial it was apparent that the second, third and eleventh articles were the ones on which the largest number would vote guilty. Accordingly, the vote was, by order of the senate, first taken on the eleventh article, there being 35 for conviction and 19 for acquittal. The senate then adjourned till May 25th, when the vote was taken on the second and third articles, with the same result. The senate then adjourned *sine die*, and the chief justice directed a verdict of acquittal to be entered upon the record.

The charges of corruption and intimidation of senators, which were so loudly made in the press, and which caused committees of investigation to be appointed in both houses, were never proven.

The seventh and last trial was that of W. W. Belknap, secretary of war under Grant. He was unanimously impeached by the house on the charge of having, for six years, received money for the appointment and retention in office of the post trader at Port Sill. Secretary Belknap had resigned, and his resignation had been accepted a few hours before the adoption of a resolution for his impeachment; and his plea was that, inasmuch as he was, both before and at the time of the adoption of the resolution of impeachment, a private citizen, the senate had no jurisdiction in the case.[1]

The house in their replication, which upheld the jurisdiction of the senate, pointed out that the respondent was an officer of the United States at the time of the commission of the acts charged, and while the investigation of his conduct was going on, his resignation being tendered with full knowledge of the proceedings and with intent to evade them.[2] Secretary Belknap denied that he had resigned in order to evade any pro-

[1] Congr. Record, 1st Sess., 44th Congr. Trial of Belknap, p. 6.

[2] *Ibid.* Trial of Belknap, p. 76.

ceedings of the house of representatives, and that the house had his case under consideration prior to his resignation, since it had neither taken any steps for the investigation of his conduct, or authorized a committee to do so ; the committee on expenditures of the war department, who had "been pretending to make some inquiry into his conduct," not having been authorized to do so, and being still engaged in examining witnesses when the house received news of his resignation.

After hearing the arguments on both sides, the question of jurisdiction was debated by the senate in secret session for thirteen days, when it was decided by a vote of 37 to 29, that Secretary Belknap was amenable to impeachment, nothwithstanding his resignation from office.[1] The counsel for defence, holding that their plea had been sustained inasmuch as two-thirds had not voted against it, refused to plead farther to the merits of the case, whereupon, in accordance with the order of the senate, the trial proceeded as on a plea of not guilty. The trial continued throughout the month of August, and when the vote was taken it stood 36 to 25 on all but the last article, on which it was 37 to 25. Belknap was accordingly acquitted.

The two trials most important in the interpretation of the constitution on the subject of impeachments are the first and last,—the first because it declared senators and representatives not to be civil officers in the meaning of the constitution, and therefore not liable to impeachment; and the last because of the position taken as to the effect of resignation upon the amenability to impeachment of the officer concerned.

At the first trial all the rules and forms of procedure for the conduct of the trial had to be decided upon, and the practices then adopted have for the most part been followed since, others being added as occasion arose.

[1] Congr. Record. Trial of Belknap, p. 76.

The rules adopted at the first trial were added to and readopted at the second and third trials, and then remained the same until the trial of President Johnson, when they underwent a complete revision.

On receipt of the articles of impeachment a summons is issued to the person accused, to appear on a certain day and answer the charges made against him. He may appear either in person or by counsel, and his answer to the articles of impeachment is at once filed. If he does not appear in either way, the trial proceeds as on a plea of not guilty. After the filing of the answer of the respondent, time is usually given for the consideration of the rejoinder, and when the court of impeachment again meets, the arguments of the counsel and managers are heard. Witnesses are examined and cross-examined in the usual way.

The rules of the first and third trials were adopted by the senate before its organization as a court of impeachment by the taking of the oath, but at the second trial not until afterwards. When the rules for the trial of President Johnson were under consideration, objection was made to their adoption before the taking of the oath, on the ground that the senate, sitting in its legislative capacity, had no right to adopt rules for governing its action as a judicial body. The objection was, however, overruled, and the rules adopted by the senate in legislative session; but they were afterwards readopted *pro forma* by the court to accord with the conviction of the chief justice on that point.[1]

Another point on which the chief justice differed from the senate was in regard to the time in the proceedings on an impeachment when the senate should be organized as a court by the taking of the oath. At the trials of Blount and Pickering, the oath was not taken until the trial was about to begin, but at the other trials

[1] Congr. Globe, 2d Sess., 40th Congr., Supplement, p. 5.

it was taken preparatory to the receipt, from the house, of the articles of impeachment. The rules adopted in 1868 provided for the administration of the oath immediately after the receipt of the articles of impeachment,[1] and it was so administered in that and the following trial, in spite of a communication of the chief justice, in which he held that not only should the taking of the oath precede the receipt of the articles of impeachment, but also the actual announcement of the impeachment.[2]

The house has always accompanied an impeachment by a demand that the senate "do take order" for the appearance of the person accused. At the first trial the senate, on the receipt of the impeachment, had held Blount in $20,000 bail; and when, on the following day, he was expelled from the senate, and his sureties gave him up, it was ordered that the messenger take him into custody "until he shall enter into recognizance himself, in the sum of $1,000, with two sufficient sureties in the sum of $500 each," which he did on the following day.[3] When the same demand was made with reference to Judge Pickering it was resolved, as in the former case: "That the Senate will take proper order thereon." No action, however, was taken, and a committee appointed at the next session to inquire if any further proceeding ought to be taken regarding the impeachment, reported that the senate had no constitutional power to take into custody the body of the person accused, and that all that was necessary was a notification to the party concerned, of the impeachment, it being optional with him whether he appeared in person, or by attorney, or not at all. The committee, therefore, held that no further proceeding should be taken by the senate, until after the receipt of the articles of impeachment.[4]

[1] Rule 3.

[2] Congr. Globe, 2d Sess., 40th Congr., p. 1644.

[3] Annals of Congress, 1st Sess., 5th Congr., p. 44.

[4] *Ibid.*, 1st Sess., 8th Congr., p. 317.

Another change is in regard to the attendance of the house. The rules adopted at the first trial provided for no accommodations for the members of the house, and there is no notice of their having attended, though the house adjourned during the progress of the trial, it being thought improper to proceed with the business of the house in the absence of so considerable a number of its members.[1] At the second trial, though preparations were made for the accommodation of the house in the senate chamber during the trial, and the house was notified of the fact, it did not adjourn during the trial, except when judgment was being pronounced, at which time it attended in the senate chamber. Since then it has always been the custom of the house to be present in the senate during the progress of the trial,[2] and the propriety of such a course of action was not questioned until the rules for regulating the procedure in the trial of President Johnson were under discussion, when it was objected to, on the ground that the presence of the house would exert an undue influence.[3] The rule was, however, adopted as usual, and the house not only attended during the trial, as in former cases, but also accompanied the managers, as a committee of the whole on the state of the union, when the articles of impeachment were presented, though their attendance at that time was not contemplated by the rules.

The rules adopted at the first trial provided for the decision with closed doors of all questions arising in the course of the trial;[4] and, under this rule, the senate had for four days debated, in secret session, the question of jurisdiction. At the next trial a step towards publicity was taken by providing for the retirement of the senate to an adjoining committee room for consideration

[1] Annals of Congress, 5th Congr., vol. III, p. 2564.

[2] In the trial of Peck they did not attend all the time.

[3] Congr. Globe, 2d Sess., 40th Congr., p. 1595.

[4] Annals of Congress, 5th Congr., vol. II, p. 2197.

of a motion, only when a third of the members present required it;[1] and, at the same time, it was agreed to admit stenographers to the trial.[2] Finally, at the trial of Judge Chase everything was made public, it being provided that "At all times whilst the Senate is sitting upon the trial of an impeachment the doors of the Senate Chamber shall be kept open." The rule remained in this form until the trial of President Johnson, when it was amended by the addition of "unless the Senate shall direct the doors to be closed while deliberating upon its decisions."[3]

At the trial of Judge Chase, provision was, for the first time, made for the publication of the proceedings on the trial. Provision was also made at the same time for the publication of the proceedings on the previous trials.[4] A proposal made at the trial of President Johnson for the reporting in confidence of the proceedings in secret session was negatived, as was also a similar proposition made at the next trial.[5]

The trial of President Johnson saw the adoption of rules for the limitation of debate. Argument on all preliminary questions was limited to one hour on each side,[6] and the final argument on the merits of the question was confined to two persons on each side.[7] It was also provided that, when the doors were closed for deliberation, no member should speak more than once on any one question, or for more than ten minutes on an introductory question, or fifteen on the final question, unless by consent of the senate to be had without debate.[8]

[1] Annals of Congress, 1st Sess., 8th Congr., p. 327.

[2] Sen. Jour., vol. III, p. 503.

[3] Rule 19.

[4] Resolution adopted February 20, 1805.

[5] Congr. Record, 1st Sess., 44th Congr., vol. IV, part vii, p. 73.

[6] *Ibid.*, 2d Sess., 44th Congr., p. 1580, Rule 20.

[7] *Ibid.*, Rule 21.

[8] As first proposed, the rule read "unless by unanimous consent;" but this was so strongly objected to that it was amended so as to read as given.

At the trial of President Johnson, the chief justice for the first time presiding, questions arose as to the extent of his powers. Though some had held that, in the trial of an impeachment, the vice president, when he presided, had a right to vote as a member, he had never exercised other than a casting vote. The same claim was made for the chief justice, but it received little support, and a motion denying his right to a casting vote was rejected by a majority of six only.

Another question was raised by the fact that there was no vice president, the question being whether, in such a case, the president *pro tempore* should be allowed to vote in the trial of the president, inasmuch as he now stood next in succession to the presidency. On this ground objection was made to his taking the oath, but, after some debate, in the course of which it was pointed out that the president *pro tempore* might be changed at any time in the course of the trial, the objection was withdrawn.[1]

[1] Congr. Globe, 2d Sess., 40th Congr., pp. 1675-1700.

## CHAPTER VI.

### CONCLUSION.

In the development of the senate, three loosely defined periods may be noted. During the first of these, which extended over about thirty years, and especially during the first half of this period, the house was the most conspicuous branch of the legislature.[1] While the legislative sessions were held in secret, it was but natural that the proceedings of the senate should attract less attention than those of the house; and that it was still so, even after the opening of the doors of the senate, may have been partly due to the force of habit; partly to the fact that the house represented the people directly, and was, therefore, more popular; and partly to the business like manner of conducting legislation in the senate,—due, doubtless, to the small number of senators and the secret sessions,—which, though conducive to good legislation, did not attract popular attention. The lack of reports of the proceedings of the senate in the papers of the day, even after the legislative sessions of the senate were made public, although those of the house were quite fully reported, would also have its influence. This being so, the house was naturally the place in which any subject was introduced, which it was desired should excite attention, and create an impression abroad. Thus it is not strange that, in spite of the executive duties entrusted to the senate, and the longer term of its members, a seat in the house was sometimes regarded as equally or even more desirable than one in the senate.[2]

[1] Morris went so far as to say that the complete sovereignty of America was substantially in the house. (Life of Morris, III, pp. 185, 186, and Diary, II, p. 528.)

[2] Madison, Works, I, 438.

Thus Clay in 1811, when there was a question of war, refused to be a candidate for re-election to the senate that he might get into the house.[1] Not only were senators occasionally seen resigning their seats to become state governors, as at present, but even to become mayors of large cities,[2] and it was by no means an unusual thing for one who had been a senator to be elected into the house of representatives.[3] In 1808 Story wrote that though the senate was ordinarily composed of men of ripe years and respectable appearance, yet the house was generally greatly superior in talents.[4] On the other hand, the *Pennsylvania Packet*, speaking of the First Congress, said: "Perhaps a more truly respectable delegation could not have been made, than appears in the Senate. Many of them are men eminently conspicuous for their abilities and political knowledge. Eleven of them were members of the Grand Convention, and were in favor of the Constitution, and they are all men in whom the people of the United States can place entire confidence for the speedy and active operation of the new government;"[5] and John Adams described the senate during his presidency, as a "select council of statesmen, true to their duties, not ambitious of logomachy, and not making their honorable station subsidiary to other objects."[6]

Most of the senators were men of moderate means,[7] and some of them were rich for that time,[8] but there

[1] Clay, Works, IV, 47.

[2] Otis, in 1821, to become mayor of Boston, and DeWitt Clinton to become mayor of New York.

[3] Webster, Works, III, 12.

[4] Life of Story, I, p. 158.

[5] Thursday, March 12th, 1789.

[6] John Adams, Works, I, 571.

[7] A Boston paper of July 8, 1789, says: "Considering that Congressmen are elected from amongst the wealthy, for their abilities and integrity," etc. (Taken from the *Pennsylvania Packet*, July 22, 1789.)

[8] Life of J. Smith, p. 57.

was not the number of wealthy men which is to be found in the senate now, and which has given it the name of "The Rich Man's Club."

The accusations of corruption, which were made even during the First Congress, are by no means proven. Hamilton, who was most frequently accused of using improper means to secure his majorities, declared that he did not know of a single senator who could properly be called a stock jobber or a paper dealer; and Madison says that the accusation of bribery in 1796 was a "slanderous assertion;"[1] while the statement of Senator Taylor, that he resigned his seat in congress because of "the extreme corruption of Congress and the President," aroused much indignation from his brother senators, who thought the statement unwarranted.[2] That there was a trading of votes is shown by the way in which the place for the capitol was decided upon.

The senate in its mode of conducting business was most orderly and dignified. A Nova Scotia paper, in 1791, said: "There is but one assembly in the whole range of the Federal Union in which eloquence is deemed unnecessary, and, I believe, even absurd and intrusive,—to-wit, the Senate, or Upper House of Congress. They are merely a deliberative meeting, in which every man delivers his concise opinion, one leg over the other, as they did in the First Congress, where an harangue was a great variety."[3] The rule, adopted in the First Congress, and still found among the rules of the senate, which provides that: "No member shall speak to another, or otherwise interrupt the business of the Senate, or read any printed paper, while the Journals or public papers are reading, or when any Senator is speaking in any

[1] Works, II, p. 71. Letter of January 10, 1796.

[2] Ames, I, 161.

[3] Taken from Sumner's Works, XIII, 191. Occasionally, however, it would seem that a "harangue" was delivered in the senate, for Maclay mentions a speech which lasted two days.

debate,"[1] was not then, as now, a dead letter, but was carefully observed. Moreover, the senators were not then accustomed to be absent from the senate chamber during a large part of the day's session; and, according to a rule given by Mr. Maclay, a senator who should withdraw from the senate chamber for more than a quarter of an hour after a quorum was formed, would be guilty of disorderly conduct, and be punished in the same way as for neglect of attendance during the session.[2]

During the latter half of the first period the legislative importance of the senate was gradually increasing, and, with the great debate over the Missouri Compromise, it obtained the lead. From that time till the civil war, the struggle between the North and South over slavery was the all important question; and this struggle was, for the most part, fought out in the senate, where, owing to the system of representation, the two sides were evenly matched. The senate thus became the center of interest for the whole country, and the place where most of the important measures were introduced, and the great debates took place which have justly gained for the senate a world wide renown. Sumner, speaking of this in 1869, said: "Without neglect of business the Senate has become a center from which to address the country. A seat here is a lofty pulpit with a mighty sounding board, and the whole wide-spread people is the congregation."[3]

The senate was still, however, remarkable for the closeness of its debates, and the brevity of its discussions, and was to be distinguished from the house by reason of its greater decorum and dignity, and the ease with which order was preserved.[4] Passions, however,

[1] Rule 2.

[2] Journal of Maclay, p. xiv, Rule 16.

[3] Sumner, Works, XIII, p. 191.

[4] Exec. Jour., V. p. 4, address of Vice President Johnson; and Benton, Thirty Years' View, I, 206–208.

sometimes ran high, it being during this period that occurred in the senate chamber that scene between Mr. Benton and Mr. Foote, in which the latter drew a pistol.

Many have borne witness to the fact that at this time the senate occupied the first place in the government. Van Buren said in 1823 that the senate, more than any other branch, controlled all the efficient power of the government; and Story, who wrote in 1833, said of the senate: "It has given a dignity, a solidity, and an enlightened spirit to the operations of government, which have maintained respect abroad and confidence at home."[1] Greeley, in 1836, said that the senate was the "ablest body of its numbers on earth";[2] and Richard Johnson, a few years later, when vice president, said: "There is not, in my opinion, upon the globe, a legislative body more respectable and more exalted in character than the Senate of the United States."[3]

The increased importance of the senate is also shown by the way in which a seat there was regarded. *Niles Register* for 1822, says: "A place in the Senate of the United States, in point of honor and respectabilty, is second only to a place in the presidential chair;"[4] and John Brown wrote to Clay ten years later that he would prefer a place in the senate to any within the reach of American ambition.[5] The highest terms of praise were made use of in regard to senators. Webster, in 1830, spoke of the senate as a "Senate of equals, of men of individual honor and personal character, and of absolute independence," who knew no master and acknowledged no dictation;[6] and De Tocqueville, who travelled in

[1] Sec. 725.

[2] Recollections of a Busy Life, p. 225.

[3] Exec. Jour., V, 4; Benton, I, 208; and Niles Register, XXII, 274, for similar statements.

[4] Vol. XXIX, p. 241.

[5] Clay, Works, IV, 343.

[6] Webster, Works, III, 274.

America in 1834, wrote regarding it: "Scarcely an individual is to be found in it, who does not recall the idea of an active and illustrious career. The Senate is composed of eloquent advocates, distinguished generals, wise magistrates, and statesmen of note, whose language would, at all times, do honor to the most remarkable parliamentary debates of Europe."[1]

During the second period, the power of the senate in nominations was much increased. At first the senate had, in the main, confined itself to the exercise of the powers, granted it by the constitution, of advising and consenting to the nominations made by the president; but, in the second period, it practically obtained, to a great extent, the power of nomination as well, a power which, owing to the great increase in the number of offices and the introduction of the spoils system, had come to be enormous. The civil service reform limited the power of the senate by decreasing the number of offices which it could control, but, except for that, its power now is as great as ever.

The new chamber, twice as large as was then needed,[2] which the senate moved into in 1859, where it was difficult for senators to make themselves heard, and the larger number of senators resulting from the admission of several new states into the union, made the senate no longer so well fitted for a debating body where the great leading questions of the day could be thoroughly discussed, and thus brought before the country. This, and the increase in the number and diversity of the subjects to be acted upon by the senate, due to the growth of the country, and the increased material prosperity which followed the war, has contributed largely to make the senate what it is in its third stage of development, when it has become more like the house, many of whose rules and practices it has adopted.

[1] Democracy in America, chap. VIII.

[2] Sumner, Works, X, 497, 498.

The senate has not, however, adopted those strict rules for the limitation of debate which are in force in the house, and it still remains the chief debating body, though it has not that preëminence in this respect which it enjoyed in the second period; its long debates, which are regarded with disfavor by the people, even when their object is not to delay business, having contributed to the loss of public esteem which the senate has suffered.

During the preceding period the minority was frequently charged by the majority with factious opposition; but it is only within recent years that minorities have not only attempted, by all sorts of factious opposition, to prevent any action to which they objected, but have boldly declared that this was their intention, and that they had a right so to do; and have followed up their declarations with sufficient persistence to gain their ends.

As all attempts by the majority in such instances to change the rules have been met by the same factious opposition, and as, when the immediate necessity for a change is passed, the majority has not shown itself eager for a change, this action of the minority has not led to the amendment of the rules, though such amendment has been loudly demanded by the country; and, as matters now stand, a very few senators, if they are only persistent and not too scrupulous, can delay indefinitely the action of the senate.

The fact that it is only recently that the opportunities for factious opposition, offered by the senate rules, have been made use of, though the rules have always been as favorable to such action as at present, would suggest that the character of the senate had degenerated. Corruption, indeed, seems to exist in the senate, as well as in every other department of government, local, state and national; for though it is seldom that the actual sale of a vote has been proven, it can scarcely be doubted that indirect means of bribery are often employed. A proposal in the second session of the Thirty-eighth Congress for a standing committee on corruption, brought out the startling fact that many reports of frauds discovered by committees had never been acted upon. That there is a good deal of corruption would also appear from the numerous proposals for its prevention, and the discussions which these have called forth.[1]

The number of rich men in the senate has increased, but the number of very rich ones who are senators only because they are rich, is often exaggerated.[2]

If, however, it is acknowledged that there is more corruption than formerly, and that the average of character of senators is lower, it is only admitting that the character of public men in general has declined; for the senate is still recruited mainly from men who have previously held some state or United States office, especially from among state governors and United States representatives, so that the senate is largely composed of the ablest men who have sat in the house. A seat in the senate, is, as a rule, preferred to one in the house, and the senate still remains the most distinguished branch of the legislature.

[1] One of the proposals most frequently made, is to forbid senators acting as attorneys for railroads.

[2] Thus Jonathan Chase said, in 1889, that fully one-half of the senators were men of small or no means, a large proportion of the others were men of moderate means, and that only a few were rich men, while there were but three or four who possessed great estates. (*North American Review*, vol. 148, p. 50.) See, also, *Forum*, "The Senate in the Light of History."

## LIST OF WORKS CITED WITH DATE AND PLACE OF PUBLICATION.

ADAMS, CHARLES FRANCIS. (See Adams, John, and Adams, J. Q.)

ADAMS, HENRY, Life of Albert Gallatin. Philadelphia, 1880.

ADAMS, HENRY, Life of John Randolph. Boston, 1883.

ADAMS, HENRY. (See Albert Gallatin.)

ADAMS, JOHN, Life and Works of. Ed. by Charles Francis Adams, 10 vols. Boston, 1856.

ADAMS, JOHN QUINCY, Memoirs of. Ed. by Charles Francis Adams, 2 vols. Philadelphia, 1874.

AMES, FISHER, Works of. Ed. by Seth Ames, 2 vols. Boston, 1854.

AMES, SETH. (See Ames, Fisher.)

ANNALS OF CONGRESS, 1st Congress—16th Congress. Washington, 1834–1855.

ATTORNEY GENERALS, Official Opinions of the, 1789–1880, 16 vols. Washington.

ATTORNEY GENERALS, Digest of Opinions of, in House Miscellaneous Documents, 2d Sess., 48th Congr., No. 3.

BENTON, THOMAS H., Thirty Years' View, 2 vols. New York, 1854.

BLAINE, JAMES G., Twenty Years of Congress, 2 vols. Norwich, Conn., 1884.

BURR, AARON. (See Davis, M. L.)

CABOT, GEORGE. (See Lodge, Henry Cabot.)

CALHOUN, JOHN C., Works of. Ed. by Richard K. Cralle, 6 vols. Vol. I, Columbia, S. C., 1851; II, 1881; III, IV, V, 1874; VI, 1879, New York.

CIVIL SERVICE COMMISSION, Reports of. Washington.

CLAY, HENRY, The Life, Correspondence, and Speeches of. Ed. by Calvin Colton, 6 vols. New York, 1857.

COLTON, CALVIN. (See Clay, Henry.)

CONGRESSIONAL DEBATES, 2d Sess., 18th Congress—1st Sess., 25th Congress, 14 vols. Washington, 1825–1837.

CONGRESSIONAL DIRECTORY. Washington, 1809, 1816, 1819–1894.

CONGRESSIONAL GLOBE, 1st Session, 23d Congress—3d Session, 42d Congress. Washington, 1834–1873.

CONGRESSIONAL RECORD, 1st Session, 43d Congress—2d Session, 53d Congress. Washington, 1874–1894.

CONKLING, ALBERT, The Life and Letters of Roscoe Conkling. New York, 1889.

CONKLING, ROSCOE. (See Conkling, Albert.)

CRALLE, RICHARD K. (See Calhoun, John C.)

DAVIS, M. L., Memoirs of Aaron Burr, 2 vols. New York, 1836.

DICKINSON, DANIEL S., Speeches, Correspondence, etc. of. Ed. by John R. Dickinson. New York, 1867.

DICKINSON, JOHN R. (See Dickinson, Daniel S.)

EATON, DORMAN B., Secret Sessions of the Senate. New York, 1886.

ELLIOT, JONATHAN, Debates on the Federal Constitution, 5 vols. Philadelphia, 1891.

EXECUTIVE JOURNAL OF THE SENATE, 1789–1828, vols. I–III, Washington, 1828. 1829–1869, vols. IV–XVI, Washington, 1887.

FEDERALIST, THE, in Works of Hamilton, Ed. by Henry Cabot Lodge, vol. IX. New York and London, 1885.

GALLATIN, ALBERT, The Writings of. Ed. by Henry Adams, 3 vols. Philadelphia and London, 1879.

GALLATIN, ALBERT. (See Stevens and Adams, Henry.)

GIBBS, GEORGE, editor of Administration of Washington and Adams, 2 vols. New York, 1846.

GREELEY, HORACE, Recollections of a Busy Life. Chicago, Cincinnati, San Francisco, Boston, New York, 1868.

GREELEY, HORACE. (See Parton.)

HALLECK, International Law, revised by Sir Sherston Baker, 2 vols. London, 1878.

HAMILTON, ALEXANDER, The Works of. Ed. by Henry Cabot Lodge, 9 vols. New York and London, 1885.

HAMILTON, ALEXANDER, The Works of. Ed. by John C. Hamilton, 7 vols. New York, 1871.

HAMILTON, JOHN C. (See Hamilton, Alexander.)

HARPER'S WEEKLY, 1870. New York.

HOUSE OF REPRESENTATIVES, Digest and Manual of. Washington.

HOUSE JOURNAL, 1789–1895. Washington.

JEFFERSON, THOMAS, Works of. Ed. by H. A. Washington, 9 vols. Philadelphia, 1869.

KENT, JAMES, Commentaries on American Law, 2d edition, 4 vols. New York, 1832.

KING, RUFUS, Life and Correspondence of. Ed. by Chas. R. King, 2 vols. New York, 1894–1895.

LODGE, HENRY CABOT, Life and Letters of George Cabot. Boston, 1878.

LODGE, HENRY CABOT. (See Hamilton, Alexander.)

MACLAY, WILLIAM, Journal of. Ed. by Edgar Maclay. New York, 1890.

MACLAY, EDGAR. (See Maclay, William.)

MCMASTER, JOHN BACH, History of the People of the United States, 3 vols. New York, 1885.

MADISON, JAMES, Writings of. Published by order of Congress, 4 vols. Philadelphia, 1867.

MANUAL. (See Senate and House.)

MORRIS, ANNE CARY. (See Morris, Gouverneur.)

MORRIS, GOUVERNEUR, The Diary and Letters of. Ed. by Anne Cary Morris, 2 vols. New York, 1888.

MORRISON, JOHN HOPKINS, Life of Jeremiah Smith. Boston, 1845.

NATION, 1865–1894. New York.

NILES REGISTER, 75 vols., 1811–1849. Baltimore.

NORTH AMERICAN REVIEW, Nos. 128, 148. New York.

PARTON, JAMES, Life of Horace Greeley. Boston, 1882.

PENNSYLVANIA PACKET. Philadelphia.

PICKERING, TIMOTHY, The Life of, 4 vols. Vol. I, ed. by Octavius Pickering, Boston, 1867; vols. II, III, IV, ed. by Charles W. Upham, Boston, 1873.

PICKERING, OCTAVIUS. (See Pickering, Timothy.)

POMEROY, JOHN NORTON, An Introduction to the Constitutional Law of the United States, 7th edition. Boston, 1883.

PUBLIC OPINION for 1893.

RANDOLPH, JOHN. (See Adams, Henry.)

RAWLE, WILLIAM, A View of the Constitution of the United States. Philadelphia, 1825.

READ, GEORGE. (See Read, William Thompson.)

READ, WILLIAM THOMPSON, Life and Correspondence of George Read. Philadelphia, 1870.

REPORTS. (See Senate and Civil Service Commission.)

REVISED STATUTES OF THE UNITED STATES. (See United States.)

SENATE EXECUTIVE DOCUMENTS, 1st Session, 30th Congress—2d Sess., 53d Congress. Washington.

SENATE JOURNAL, 1789–1815, reprint in 5 vols. Vols. I–II, 1820; vols. III–V, 1821. 1815–1895, Washington.

SENATE MISCELLANEOUS DOCUMENTS, 1st Session, 30th Congress—2d Session, 53d Congress. Washington.

SENATE PUBLIC DOCUMENTS, 1st Session, 18th Congress—2d Session, 29th Congress. Washington.

SENATE, Reports of Committees of the, 1st Session, 30th Congress—2d Session, 53d Congress. Washington.

SENATE, STATE PAPERS, 3d Session, 13th Congress—2d Session, 17th Congress. Washington.

SMITH, JEREMIAH. (See Morrison, John Hopkins.)

SPARKS, JARED, Life of Gouverneur Morris, 3 vols. Boston, 1832.

SPARKS, JARED. (See Webster, Daniel.)

STATUTES AT LARGE. (See United States.)

STEVENS, JOHN AUSTIN, Life of Albert Gallatin. Boston, 1884.

STORY, JOSEPH, Life and Letters of. Ed. by William W. Story. 2 vols. Boston, 1851.

STORY, JOSEPH, Commentaries on the Constitution, 3d edition, 2 vols. Boston, 1833.

STORY, WILLIAM. (See Story, Joseph.)

SUMNER, CHARLES, Memoirs and Letters of. 15 vols. Boston, 1870–1883.

SUPPLEMENT TO REVISED STATUTES. (See United States.)

SUPREME COURT. (See United States.)

TIMES, New York Daily, 1860, 1861, 1869.

TREATIES AND CONVENTIONS between the United States and Other Powers, 1776–1887. Washington, 1889.

TRIBUNE, New York Semi-Weekly, 1861.

UNITED STATES, Reports of the Circuit Court.

UNITED STATES, Reports of the Supreme Court.

UNITED STATES, Revised Statutes, 2d edition. Washington, 1878.

UNITED STATES, Statutes at Large, 1789–1887, 24 vols. Washington.

UNITED STATES, Supplement to the Revised Statutes of. Vol. I, 1874–1891. Washington, 1891. Vol. II, 1892–1893. Washington, 1893.

UPHAM, CHARLES W. (See Pickering, Timothy.)

WASHINGTON, GEORGE, Writings of. Ed. by Worthington Chauncey Ford, 13 vols. New York and London, 1889.

WASHINGTON, W. A. (See Jefferson, Thomas.)

WEBSTER, DANIEL, The Works of. Ed. by Jared Sparks, 6 vols. Boston, 1851.

WHEATON, HENRY, Elements of International Law. Ed. by Richard Henry Dana, 8th edition. Boston, 1866.

WILLIAMS'S Statesman's Manual, 2 vols. New York, 1846.

WINSOR, JUSTIN, editor of Narrative and Critical History of the United States, 8 vols. Boston and New York, 1887–89.

# INDEX.

www.ingramcontent.com/pod-product-compliance
Lightning Source LLC
Chambersburg PA
CBHW030832270326
41928CB00007B/1009

*9783337150969*